SO-CFX-688

THE INTERNET
QUICK REFERENCE

Bill Eager

201 West 103rd Street, Indianapolis, Indiana 46290

THE INTERNET QUICK REFERENCE

ISBN: 0-7897-2028-0

International ISBN: 0-7897-2087-6

Library of Congress Catalog Card Number: 99-61236

Printed in the United States of America

First Printing: June 1999

01   00   99   4   3   2   1

TRADEMARKS

WARNING AND DISCLAIMER

Executive Editor Jim Minatel	**Managing Editor** Thomas F. Hayes	**Proofreader** Maribeth Echard
Acquisitions Editor Stephanie J. McComb	**Project Editor** Damon Jordan	**Interior Design** Louisa Klucznik
Development Editor Stacia Mellinger	**Copy Editor** Kay Hoskin	**Cover Design** Dan Armstrong
Technical Editor Mark Hall	**Indexer** Kevin Kent	**Layout Technician** Jeannette McKay

SECTION I

KICKSTART

1

The Internet continues to blast off. Today, approximately 50 million people have access to the Net, with projections for approximately 178 million users by the year 2002. If these numbers prove true, that's an incredible 89,887 new users every day for the next four years! In fact, it is amazing how quickly the Internet has become a mass medium. In four years, the Internet has grown to reach an audience of 50 million users—it took radio 38 years to achieve this audience size.

The other aspect of the Internet that is not slowing down is the speed of access. Fighting the phrase "world wide wait," cable companies, telephone companies, and Internet service providers (ISPs) continue to offer faster access speeds.

It might seem obvious, but if you want to use the Internet you need three things—a computer, Internet access, and Internet software. What is not so obvious is what type of computer, access, or software you should get and where to get it. The following subsections provide information on these topics. Specifically, this section addresses the following main topic areas:

- Computer Requirements for Internet Access
- Internet Access Providers
- Internet Software

COMPUTER REQUIREMENTS FOR INTERNET ACCESS

What type of computer hardware do you need to get to use the Internet? Every day it seems there is a newer, faster computer advertised on television. You might already have a perfectly adequate PC for using the Internet. The following are minimum requirements for a PC that you want to use on the Internet:

- **Computer**   486/66 or higher, 16MB of memory (RAM), CD-ROM drive, 80MB of hard disk space available

- **Operating system**   Windows 95 or Windows 98
- **A modem**   28.8Kbps modem (56Kbps is preferred)

If your computer doesn't have these minimum requirements, you will find that using the Internet is not a pleasurable experience because it will be very slow. The speed at which you surf the Net depends upon more than just your modem (although that is a big factor). A faster processor and additional RAM also improve the speed at which Web pages are processed on your desktop. If you're purchasing a new computer, make certain that it has a 56Kbps modem.

INTERNET ACCESS PROVIDERS

The options in terms of how to get onto the Internet continue to increase, which is good for us Internet users. There are several different types of companies that you can use to get Internet access. All these companies can be referred to as Internet service providers (ISPs) because they are providing Internet service to you. The types of companies include the following:

- **Local Internet service providers (ISPs)**   These are companies in your town or city that are in the business of providing Internet access for consumers and businesses.
- **National Internet service providers**   These are companies that sell Internet access to people across the country. Sometimes these national ISPs have local phone numbers that you call to access the Internet, and sometimes they offer 800 numbers. America Online and The Microsoft Network are examples of national ISPs.
- **Cable companies**   An increasing number of cable companies are offering Internet access to their customers. Unlike the local and national ISPs, the access is provided over the coaxial cable.
- **Phone companies**   Yes, regional and local phone companies are quickly getting into the business of providing Internet access.

The upcoming subsections provide more in-depth detail on
Internet access options by the various Internet service
providers. Sometimes the choices seem overwhelming.
Choose a provider based on price, customer service, and
the access speed that you need.

Local Internet Service Providers

There are literally thousands of local ISPs across the
country (and around the world). These companies are
usually located in your town, or a nearby town. They can
be found in the Yellow Pages under an Internet heading.
One advantage of a local ISP is that usually they are more
responsive to your questions and provide better customer
service. Some are good, some are not. Ask your friends who
have access which ISP they recommend.

In addition, you can ask different local ISPs some of the
following questions in an effort to determine how equipped
each would be in serving your needs:

- How many customers do you have?
- What is your ratio of customers per modem? (They
  shouldn't have more than about 10 customers per
  modem at their facility.)
- What modem speeds do you support? (Remember, you
  want 56Kbps.)
- What are your hours of customer service?
- Can I host my Web site as part of my access account?
- How much disk space do I get?
- How many email boxes can I have?
- When I am on the road, is there a toll-free number to
  dial in and what are the charges?
- What software (Web browser, email, FTP) do you
  provide?

If you're already on the Internet but are thinking of switch-
ing to another provider, try the CNET Web site at
`www.cnet.com/Content/Reports/Special/ISP/index.html` to
locate a local ISP and see how other users grade them.

Today, it should be standard to offer 56Kbps access. You can search for local and national ISPs by name or state at the CNET Web site.

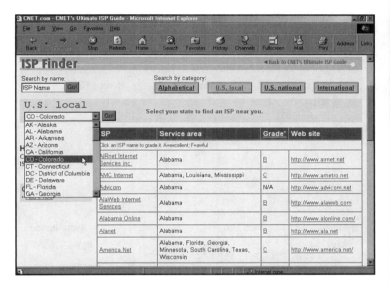

National Internet Service Providers

National Internet service providers provide Internet access across most, if not all, of the United States. Thus, they are national providers. Unlike a local ISP that might have hundreds or thousands of customers, these companies have millions of customers. This isn't necessarily a good or bad thing. Many of these offer a flat, per-month fee for unlimited access. Usually they have a local phone number for you to dial into the Internet. They might have additional per-minute charges if you are not in one of the towns or cities where they have a dial-in phone number. If this is the case, they will offer an 800 number with additional per-minute charges.

There are both advantages and disadvantages to national ISPs. One advantage is that because they are national, if you travel you can often access your account through a local number in the city you are in. Many of the national ISPs offer either an online community (a place for people who have signed up to communicate with one another) or Web site with special information and features for members. Sometimes it is more difficult to get online (but not always).

With some 16 million customers, America Online is certainly one of the most well-known national ISPs. Prices for Internet access seem to change every month. So, the best advice is to call a couple of the national ISPs listed in Table 1 to see what they currently offer. If you find one that suits your budget and offers the access speed you want, they will send you the software you need to both get onto the Internet and use it.

Table 1 provides a list of well-known national ISPs.

Table 1

National ISPs

National ISP	Web Site	Phone Number
America Online	http://www.aol.com	800-827-6364
AT&T Worldcom	http://www.att.net	800-967-5363
CompuServe	http://www.compuserve.com	800-848-8990
GTE	http://www.gte.com	888-483-6381
MCI Worldcom	http://www.mciworldcom.com	800-444-3333
Microsoft Network	http://www.msn.com	800-386-5550
Prodigy	http://www.prodigy.com	800-776-3449
PSINet	http://www.psinet.com	518-283-8860
Netcom	http://www.netcom.com	800-638-2661
Sprint	http://www.sprint.com	800-746-3767

Following are a few questions you might want to ask when you sign up:

- Is there a local phone number in my town?
- If I travel, in which cities do you have local phone numbers?

- Is there a flat, per-month fee for unlimited access?
- If there are additional per-minute charges, what are they and when do they apply?
- What connection speed can I get (28.8Kbps, 56Kbps, or higher)?
- Do you have an online site or Web site with special services for members?
- What are the hours of your technical support and is this number toll free?
- What are the customer-to-modem ratios?

WebTV

Microsoft owns the WebTV Network. WebTV is a set-top device that you attach to your television set to view and access the Internet via the TV set. You also connect the WebTV box to your phone line to dial into the Internet. WebTV offers both a handheld remote and a wireless keyboard. WebTV has a built-in modem and a small computer that actually stores many of the Web pages that you visit. The single biggest advantage to WebTV is that it brings the Internet into the comfort of your living room. Now, instead of sitting in your study, you can surf the Web from your couch. WebTV also offers some value-added services such as the capability to get a daily directory of TV listings, to easily switch between the TV and the Internet, watch TV and navigate the Internet simultaneously, and to access Web sites for local information and service. You can quickly access information about local news, weather, dining, and entertainment. You also get a WebTV email address when you sign up. WebTV offers access speeds of 28.8 and 56Kbps.

WebTV is sold at most electronics and computer stores. If you need more information about the WebTV Network, visit www.webtv.com or call 800-469-3288. Depending on the model and service you select, prices for WebTV range from $99 to $199 and the monthly fee ranges from $19.95 to $24.95.

Cable Modems

That's right, the same company that brings you cable television might now offer high-speed Internet access. Cable modems are fast and provide downstream speeds of between 1 and 5Mbps (that's megabits per second). This provides speed that can be 100 times faster than a 56Kbps modem. North American cable operators are expected to have more than one million cable modem subscribers by the end of 1999. These operators now add an average of more than 1,000 installations per day.

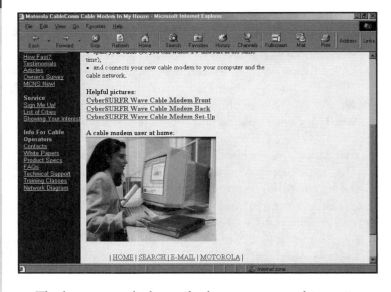

The best way to find out whether you can get this service is to call your local cable operator. If you can get the service, the operator needs to install a cable modem for your PC and a special line from the cable to your PC. There are several national cable services. @Home (www.home.com) and RoadRunner (www.rr.com) offer their services in more than 50 cities. The average monthly price for cable modem service is $40 per month and you can usually rent or buy the cable modem.

Cable modems have both downstream and upstream speeds. Downstream refers to the speed of service from the Internet to your PC. This is the speed that counts when you click a Web page and want it to load fast. Upstream is the speed from your PC to the network. This can be much slower because you are generally not sending a lot of information back to the network. But, if you are getting Internet access for a business environment, you might want fast upstream as well to send files to your customers. Or, if you are going to use two-way video conferencing, it is helpful to have high speeds in both directions.

One thing to find out is whether the service is *telco-return* or *two-way*. With telco-return you use the cable modem for the downstream service and your phone line (telco-return) for the upstream. Two-way service provides both downstream and upstream service through the cable. The disadvantage to telco-return is that you tie up your phone line when you are online.

Following are a few questions you might ask when signing up:

- Can I lease the cable modem or must I buy it?
- What is the minimum rate of downstream speed that you guarantee?

INTERNET ACCESS PROVIDERS

- Is this service telco-return or two-way?
- What are your hours of customer service?
- Can I host a Web site on your service?
- Because cable modem speeds depend on the amount of cable modem users, you might want to ask about a guaranteed rate of service.

One reason that you might not want to purchase the cable modem is because today not all cable modems and systems are standardized. This means that if you buy a cable modem and move to another city, the cable modem might not work on the new system.

NOTE

Many of the new computers are cable-modem ready. This does not mean that they have a cable modem, only that they have an Ethernet port—a special high-speed interface—that makes it very easy to add the cable modem to your PC.

Digital Subscriber Lines

Digital Subscriber Lines, also known as xDSL (because there are several choices), encompass a variety of technologies and access options that enable you to have high-speed access over standard telephone lines. These DSL services are offered by telephone companies including the Regional Bell Operating Companies such as US WEST and Bell South. Other companies, including some of the local and national ISPs, are now getting into business to provide DSL services.

What can be confusing is that there are several different versions of DSL available including HDSL (High Bit Rate DSL), SDSL (Single Line DSL), RADSL (Rate Adaptive DSL), ADSL (Asymmetric DSL), and VDSL (Very High Bit Rate DSL). Each of these offers slightly different speeds. ADSL is very popular and supports data rates from 1.5 to 9Mbps downstream (to your PC) and from 16 to 640Kbps upstream (from your PC).

One advantage of the xDSL service is that you can use one phone line to simultaneously access the Internet to have telephone conversations. Another advantage is that the speed of the connection does not slow down if other users go online (which can happen with cable modems). One of the limitations of xDSL is that users must be within 18,000 feet of a telephone company central office.

The best way to find out whether you can get one of the xDSL services is to contact your local telephone company. However, many **Internet service providers** now offer xDSL, also. If you are thinking about getting high-speed Internet access with DSL, it is worth making a few calls to your phone company and other local ISPs to see whether they offer it. xDSL has both downstream and upstream speeds.

Inexpensive Internet Access

What if you only want to occasionally surf the Web, and still have an email account without the expense of Internet access? Don't despair. Increasingly, there are places to access the Internet outside of the home. In fact, there is a Burger King on Broadway in New York City that lets you surf the Net after you buy lunch! Cybercafés, which offer food, drinks, and Internet access, are popping up all over the world. You can visit a cybercafé in Kuwait at www.ole.com.kw.

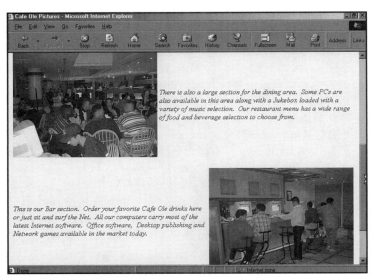

Table 2 provides a few ideas for places you might find inexpensive, if not free, Internet access. After you have the access, you can go to one of the Web-based email services to set up your email account. Then, you are set with access and email for a minimal fee. This is also a good way to see whether you like what the Internet has to offer.

Table 2
Where to Find Inexpensive Internet Access

Location	Type of Internet Access
Airports	Internet kiosks to quickly check email and access the Web
Copy center	Self-service, pay-by-the-hour
Cybercafé	Coffeehouses with Internet access
Library	Internet terminals
Retail outlets	Stores that have kiosks

Clearly the pros of these services is that they offer an inexpensive way to use the Internet. What are the downsides? You might have to wait in line if someone else is using the service. And they might not offer access to certain Internet services (such as newsgroups).

INTERNET SOFTWARE

One of the great things about the Internet is that you don't need to buy any software. Your Internet service provider provides you with the software you need to connect to and use the Internet. (Typically, connection involves using the dial-up networking program that comes with Windows 95 and Windows 98.) If your ISP doesn't have its own proprietary software (such as America Online), it usually provides you with either Netscape Navigator or Microsoft Internet Explorer. Both of these browser software programs come with everything you need to view Web sites, access newsgroups, and use email—the three big applications of the Internet. However, even if you get these programs, you might want to periodically check both Netscape and

Microsoft to see whether they have a new version of their browser available for download from their Web site.

If you want to expand your collection of Internet software, there are a few other software programs that you might consider. For example, in addition to email, newsgroup, and browser services, you might want software for FTP (file transfer protocol) that makes it easy to upload and download files from your hard drive to other computers. This comes in handy when you are building a Web site and need to transfer files to the host computer. A file compression/uncompression program can make it easier to send large files to your friends. Most of the companies that make these programs offer free versions or trials that you can download from their Web site.

Table 3 provides a list of the different types of Internet programs that you can use for different applications (such as email or Web browser).

Table 3

Internet Software

Software	Description	Web Site
Web Browsers (with Email and Newsreaders)		
Netscape Communicator	Browser	`www.netscape.com`
Internet Explorer	Browser	`www.microsoft.com/ie/`
Email		
Eudora	A popular email program	`www.eudora.com`
Pegasus	Support for multiple users	`www.pegasus.usa.com`
Newsreader		
Freeagent	A newsgroup reader	`www.forteinc.com`
FTP		
CuteFTP	A Windows-based FTP program	`www.cuteftp.com`

continues

Table 3   Continued
Internet Software

Software	Description	Web Site
WSFTP	A good FTP program	`www.ipswitch.com`
File Compression		
WinZip	A file-compression program	`www.winzip.com`
Personalized News		
PointCast	News, stocks, weather on your desktop	`www.pointcast.com`

ELECTRONIC MAIL

Electronic mail (email) is the single most popular application of the Internet. How popular? Every single minute, five million (that's *MILLION*) email messages are sent. That adds up to a total of 2.7 trillion emails last year. Email is popular because it offers a convenient way to send messages and files to people very quickly. This section provides quick reference on how to use three of the most popular email programs—America Online, Microsoft Outlook Express, and Netscape Communicator. Also, you will learn how to get and use a free Web-based email account at Hotmail. You can compose, send, and receive email messages directly from this Web site. Other more general email concepts are touched on as well. Specifically, this section addresses the following main-topic areas:

- Email Addresses
- Internet Acronyms and Smileys
- Using America Online
- Using Hotmail
- Using Netscape Messenger
- Using Outlook Express
- Web-Based Email

EMAIL ADDRESSES

Just as you have an address for your house or apartment, you need a specific address to send and receive email. You can get an email address from your Internet service provider (ISP) when you sign up for Internet access. An ISP is the company that helps you get on the Internet—they can be local or national. Or you can get a free email address from one of the Web-based email services (where you do not need to sign up for Internet access—see "Web-Based Email" and "Using Hotmail").

Email addresses are broken down into three sections:

1. Username
2. @ (translated "at")
3. Name of the host computer that receives and sends your mail

For example: eager@rmi.net or santaclaus@aol.com

Sometimes an email address can give you a little information about the user. The very last part of an email address (the .net or .com) is known as a top-level domain. The top-level domain simply refers to how the company that provides the email service to the user has registered their computer network on the Internet. These domain names either define the type of organization or the geographic location of the address. For organizational names, there are seven top-level domains (see Table 4).

Table 4
Organizational Top-Level Domains

Name	Type of Organization
Com	Commercial
Edu	Educational
Gov	Government
Int	International
Mil	Military
Net	Network
Org	Organization (commonly nonprofit groups)

Because the world of the Internet is rapidly running out of addresses (especially .com), there might soon be additional organizational domains added (see Table 5).

18

EMAIL ADDRESSES

Table 5

Possible Additional Organizational Domains

Name	Type of Organization
Arts	Cultural and arts
Firm	Business
Info	Information services
Nom	Personal names
Rec	Recreational
Store	Stores
Web	Organizations related to the Web

The geographic top-level domains are abbreviations that identify the country where the host computer resides. So an address such as beager@bingo.com.mx would be in Mexico (because mx is the country code for Mexico). In the United States, we do not use the final .us on our email addresses. There are lots of country codes and sometimes they are obvious, sometimes not (see Table 6).

Table 6

Geographic Top-Level Domains

Country	Country Code
Canada	ca
China	cn
Great Britain	uk
France	fr
Germany	de
Mexico	mx
Switzerland	ch
United States	us

> **TIP**
>
> Need to find a country code (or learn what one is)? You can find a great Web site at `www.candw.to/codes.htm` where you can click any letter of the alphabet to locate all the country codes that begin with that letter.

INTERNET ACRONYMS AND SMILEYS

Anyone in their right mind would agree that the world has too many acronyms. This does not prevent people from creating an ever-increasing number of acronyms. And, on the Internet, acronyms can actually help as a kind of short-hand when emailing. However, it gets a little crazy when you have no idea what the acronym means. Check out Table 7 for some help.

Table 7

Internet Acronyms

Acronym	What It Means
24/7	24 hours a day, 7 days a week
ACK	Acknowledgment
AWHFY	Are We Having Fun Yet
AYT	Are You There
B4	Before
BTDT	Been There Done That
BTW	By The Way
C&P	Copy & Paste
CUL	See You Later
FAQ	Frequently Asked Question
FYI	For Your Information
GOK	God Only Knows

continues

Table 7   Continued

Internet Acronyms

Acronym	What It Means
H&K	Hugs & Kisses
JMO	Just My Opinion
L8R	Later
MYOB	Mind Your Own Business
NIMBY	Not In My Back Yard
RTS	Read The Screen
SWAK	Sealed With A Kiss
QPQ	Quid Pro Quo
TWIS	That's What I Said
WB	Welcome Back
WYSIWYG	What You See Is What You Get
Y2K	Year 2000

TIP

Need more acronyms? A Web site that explains hundreds of these acronyms is found at `http://members.aol.com/nigthomas/alphabet.html`.

A Smiley enables you to use some of the characters on your keyboard to signify emotion in your email messages. Smileys are also popular in online chat sessions. You view a Smiley sideways. Some Smileys are really easy to see and understand; others are harder. There are no rules to Smileys, so make up some of your own. Check out Table 8.

Table 8

The Smileys

Smiley	Meaning
: -)	Happy face
; -)	Wink, like what you say is a little joke
: - (	Frown
: - I	Indifferent
(: - *	Kiss
(: - &	Anger
: - X	Your lips are sealed
: - o	Uh oh
(- :	Left-handed
8 -)	Wearing sunglasses

TIP

Need more Smileys? Get a good list at `www.cg.tuwien.ac.at/~helwig/smileys.html`

USING AMERICA ONLINE

With more than 16 million users around the world, America Online (AOL) is the largest online service. AOL offers its users, or members, a variety of functions that include content that is only available on AOL, the Web, newsgroups, and electronic mail (email).

The upcoming subsections offer detailed instruction for performing tasks relating to AOL as an email service.

Quick Tips		
Feature	*Button*	*Keyboard Shortcut*
Read Mail		Ctrl+R
Write Mail		Ctrl+M
Send Mail		Alt+M+S
Address Book		Alt+M+A
Mail Preferences		Alt+M+P
Mail Extras		Alt+M+E
Spell Check		Ctrl+=
Dictionary		Alt+E+D
Thesaurus		Alt+E+H

Check and Read Email

Each time you sign on to America Online, the Welcome Page provides a little logo that indicates when you have new mail "You Have Mail," and if your speakers are turned on, you will hear the now famous "You Have Mail." To retrieve your mail, perform the following steps:

1. Click the **You Have Mail** icon in the Welcome window or click the **Read** button on the toolbar.
2. New mail appears in the New Mail window (you see the date of the message, who sent it, and the title of their message).
3. Double-click the message to retrieve it.
4. Click **Next** to view the next message.

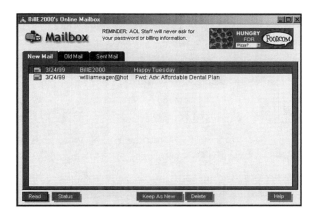

TIP

Junk email. Avoiding junk email is difficult. That doesn't mean that you have to read it. Look at the email addresses that are sending you mail. If you don't recognize the address, it's probably junk email. The subjects of messages can sometimes tell you if the mail is junk mail. Messages that use words or phrases such as "free" or "make money fast" are easy to spot. Other times it's more difficult as the junk mailer uses a phrase such as "see you tonight" and you might think it's from someone you know. See "Control Junk Email" for more ideas.

Reply to a Message

To reply to a message you have received, perform the following steps:

1. Open the message you want to reply to (see the section "Check and Read Email").

2. Click the **Reply** button.

3. Type your message in the Message window and click the **Send Now** or **Send Later** button.

Forward a Message

To forward a message you have received, perform the following steps:

1. Open the message you want to forward (see the section "Check and Read Email").

2. Click the **Forward** button.

3. Type the address of the person (or people) to whom you want to forward this message.

4. Type your message in the Message window and click the **Send Now** or **Send Later** button.

Save a Message

To save a message you have received, perform the following steps:

1. Open the email message you want to save (see section "Check and Read Email").

2. Choose **File**, then **Save**.

3. Type a filename.

4. Select the directory you want the file to be saved to.

5. Click **Save**. The message is saved as a text file in the specified directory.

Compose and Send Email

To create a new message and to send it, perform the following steps:

1. Click the **Write** button on the toolbar, which opens the Write Mail window.

2. In the Send To box, type the email address of your recipient (if you are sending to more than one person, separate the email addresses with a comma). Or, click the **Address Book** to use a stored email address (see "Create Addresses for the Address Book").

3. If you are sending a copy of the message to someone, enter their address in the Copy To field.

4. In the Subject field, enter the subject of your message.

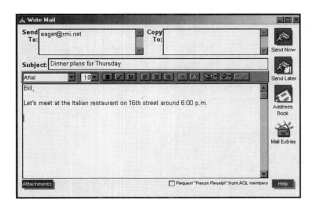

5. Type your message in the Message window.

6. Click the **Send Now** or **Send Later** button. (**Send Later** allows you to queue your outgoing mail to send at any time you want. The advantage is that you might decide to add to or change your email before you actually send it.)

Add an Attachment

One great aspect of email is that you can send people more than just words. You can attach files to your email messages. Appropriately referred to as attachments, these files can really be anything: digital photographs, word processing files, spreadsheets, or sound files. The person to whom you send the attachment can then view, read, listen to, or use your file. To add an attachment to a message you are creating, perform the following steps:

1. Click the **Write** 📝 button on the toolbar, which opens the Write Mail window.

2. Click the **Attachments** button.

3. Click **Attach**.

4. Locate the file on your hard drive that you want to attach.

5. Click **Open**.

6. Click **OK**, or **Attach** to add another attachment.

> **TIP**
>
> Knowing whether the person you are sending an attachment to can actually use your file is important. There are many versions of software programs, and sometimes the earlier versions cannot read files created with the most recent versions. Before you send your attachment, ask (in an email letter) the person that you are sending it to whether they have a program that will open your file.

Insert a Picture in Your Email

If you know that your recipient is another AOL user, you can insert a picture in your message. (If not, many email programs will not show pictures inserted into a message. You can, however, always attach a picture file to your mail message.) To insert a picture in your email message, perform the following steps:

1. Click the **Write** button on the toolbar, which opens the Write Mail window.
2. Click the **Camera** button, then **Insert a Picture**.
3. Locate the picture on your hard drive, and click **OK**.
4. If the picture is too large for the mail screen, AOL asks if you would like to resize the image to fit in the document. Click **Yes, Resize the Image** and the image is automatically resized and pasted into your email message.

Create an Email Address Book

After you use email for a little while, you'll start to gather a large list of friends, family, and colleagues who have email addresses. Most email programs enable you to save a list of people with their email addresses in an electronic address book. Open this address book and you can quickly select one or more people to whom to send your messages. Another popular option of email address books is the capability to save address information for a group of people— email addresses for more than one person that are collectively saved under one entry in your address book. (For example, you might want to save a list of all the people in your car pool in a group called CarPool.) To create your address book, perform the following steps:

1. Click the **Mail Center** button 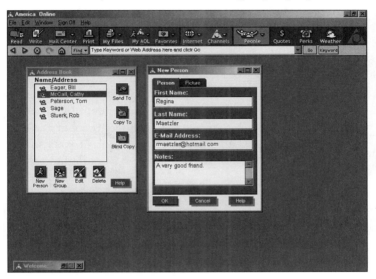 on the toolbar.
2. Select **Address Book**.
3. Click either the **New Person** icon or the **New Group** icon depending upon whether you are creating an address book entry for one individual or a group of people.

4. Enter a first name, last name, and email address.
5. Click **OK**.

Locate Addresses for Other AOL Members

With AOL, you can actually search for other members' email addresses. Perform the following steps:

1. Click the **People** button on the toolbar, then **Search AOL Member Directory**.
2. From the Quick Search tab, type the name of the person you want to find in the field labeled Member Name.
3. Click the **Search** button.
4. Scroll down the list of names that appears in the results window.
5. Double-click any of the names in the results window to access a more detailed profile of the user. Part of that detailed profile is the user's email address.

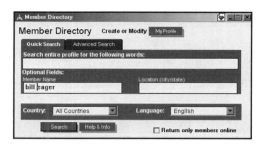

Control Junk Email

America Online enables you to establish some filters to control the mail that comes in and goes out from specific AOL screen names. A screen name is the identification for members of America Online. For example, you can allow only other AOL members to send you email, or you can block email from certain people or Web sites. Perform the following steps:

1. Click the **Mail Center** button on the toolbar.
2. Select **Mail Controls**.
3. Click **Set Up Mail Controls**.
4. Select the screen name for which you want to modify mail controls and click **Edit**.
5. Choose the settings that you prefer to control incoming and outgoing mail.

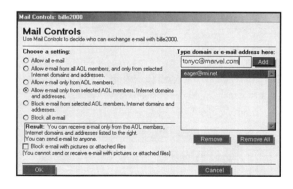

USING HOTMAIL

Microsoft owns Hotmail. Perhaps this is one reason that, with more than 10 million subscribers, Hotmail is the world's largest provider of free Web-based email. *Newsweek* magazine notes, "Hotmail is the biggest free email service provider around—with good reason. Hotmail's controls are the easiest and most intuitive of all those we looked at." (For additional Web-based email, see "Web-Based Email" near the end of this main section on electronic mail.)

The upcoming subsections offer detailed instruction for performing tasks relating to Hotmail as an email service.

Set Up Your Hotmail Account

The first thing you need to do to use Hotmail is establish your free account. To do so, perform the following steps:

1. Go to the Hotmail homepage at `www.hotmail.com`. (Notice that if you are already a Hotmail user (or member) you enter your login name and password and jump right in.) (You have the choice of using Hotmail either with frames or without them.)

2. Click the **Sign Up Here!** button on the homepage.

3. Click **I Accept** at the next page, the Terms of Agreement.

4. At the registration page, select your login name (which is also your Hotmail email address). For example, `williameager@hotmail.com`.

5. Select your password and answer the other questions on this registration page (your state, zip code, year of birth, and so forth).

6. Click **OK**.

7. The next page confirms your account and asks you to enter both your login name and password to make sure everything works. This page also asks for a password hint question and answer. Hotmail uses this question if you ever forget your password. For example, the question could be "What is my dog's name?" and then you provide the answer.

8. Click **OK**. The good news is that you only have to register for Hotmail one time. After this initial registration, you simply log in at the home page.

NOTE

You will have to log into your Hotmail account at least once within ten (10) days of creating your account, and at least once every 120 days thereafter to keep your account active.

TIP

Frequently, you'll find that someone else has already taken your first choice for a login name. Sometimes if you use your entire name (including middle initial), you will be the only person with that selection.

Log In to Hotmail

Logging in to Hotmail is easy. Perform the following steps:

1. Go to the Hotmail home page at **www.hotmail.com**.
2. Type your login name and password.
3. Click the ⏎Enter button.

Retrieve Your Password

So, what happens if you forget your Hotmail password (see "Set Up Your Hotmail Account")? No worries. Perform the following steps:

1. Click the **Forgot Your Password?** icon on the Hotmail home page.
2. Type your login name and Click **OK**.
3. Type the answer to the password retrieval question that you set up when you registered (see "Set Up Your Hotmail Account"). Click **OK**.
4. Your password is retrieved.

Check and Read Email

Every time you log in to Hotmail (see "Log In to Hotmail"), the Hotmail Welcome Page becomes your first screen.

New—identifies any new messages with a little red arrow

Check box—selects messages for moving or deleting

From—shows whom the message is from

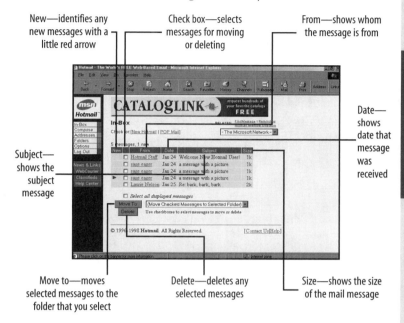

Subject— shows the subject message

Date— shows date that message was received

Move to—moves selected messages to the folder that you select

Delete—deletes any selected messages

Size—shows the size of the mail message

All new email messages are displayed onscreen here when you log in. To read an individual message, perform the following steps:

1. Click the subject line for any message you want to read.

2. The email message opens and displays onscreen.

Reply to and Forward Messages

To reply to or to forward a message you have received, perform the following steps:

1. Open the message you want to reply to or forward (see previous section).

2. Immediately below the Date: line, the message toolbar offers a Reply and Forward button. Click the button you want.

3. Enter mail addresses in the **To:** field accordingly.

4. Click the **Send** button.

Create Folders for Mail Messages

After you use Hotmail for a while, you'll start to accumulate lots of messages. So, you'll need to start organizing the messages into folders. To create folders for mail messages, perform the following steps:

1. Click **Folders** from the main navigation window.

2. Click the **Create** link.

3. Enter a name in the New Folder Name field.

4. Click **OK**.

NOTE

Hotmail starts you with several standard folders for mail organization. These include Inbox, Sent Messages, Drafts, and Trash Can. To manage messages that are in a specific folder, you first click the name of the Folder in the Folder screen, and then you can read, delete, or move the messages. The Trash Can folder is emptied automatically several times per week and messages in your trash do not count toward your account limit.

Organize Messages

After you start accumulating messages with Hotmail, you'll probably want to organize them in folders. You can move and organize messages in specially created folders (see previous section) and in the standard folders (for example, Drafts). To move messages from one folder to another (in this case, from the Inbox folder to a different folder), perform the following steps:

1. Go to the **Inbox** screen. (The Inbox screen is the first screen you get to when you log into Hotmail; you can also go directly to this screen at any time by clicking on the Inbox icon).

2. Click the check box next to the message(s) you want to move.

3. At the bottom of the Inbox screen, click the drop-down menu that lists message folders (these include Sent Messages, Drafts, and Trash Can). Select one of these folders.

4. Click the **Move To** button.

Compose and Send Email

To create a new message and to send it, perform the following steps:

1. Click the **Compose** button on the Navigation bar. The Compose mail screen appears.

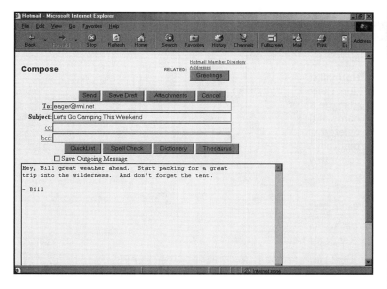

2. Enter a valid email address in the To: field (use either a comma or a space if you put in more than one address).

3. Enter a subject for your message in the Subject: field.

4. Enter your message in the Message area.

5. Click the **Send** button to send your email message.

NOTE

When you write a message, you might want to save what you have and complete and send the message at a later time. Here's where the Save Draft feature comes in handy. Click Save Draft and your message is saved in the Save Draft folder where you can access and finish the message at any time.

Add Links, HTML, and Images to Messages

You can include links to other Web sites (hyperlinks), and embed HTML code and images in your Hotmail messages. Any person who uses Hotmail (or other mail software that can read HTML) will see your links as hyperlinks in the message. Your HTML code will be viewed and your pictures will be embedded in the message. To add a hyperlink to a Web site or page, simply write the complete Web address in the format **www.espn.com**. HTML code enables you to select fonts, font colors, and sizes that your recipient will see. For example, if you wrote `<b>Hello</b>`, the word `Hello` would be in bold. If you do use HTML in your message, be sure to start your HTML with the `<html>` tag and end the message with the `</html>` tag. To add a picture to a message, follow the steps in the following section. The image must be either a GIF or JPEG file for the reader to see it onscreen.

Add an Attachment

If you are using Microsoft Internet Explorer version 4.0 or better or Netscape Navigator 2.0 or better, you can attach a file from your hard drive to a message. You can send any type of file, but the total size for all attachments cannot exceed 1 megabyte. To add an attachment to a message you are creating, perform the following steps:

1. Go to the Compose page by clicking **Compose** in the Navigation window.

2. From the Compose page, click the **Attachments** button.

3. From the Attachments page, click the **Browse** button to open a Windows directory tree for your hard drive.

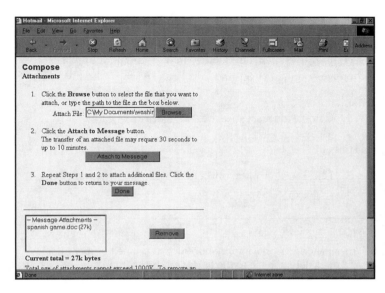

4. Select the file you want to attach to your message (or type the path and name of the file into the Attach File: textbox).

5. Click the **Attach to Message** button.

6. Repeat steps 3, 4, and 5 to attach additional files.

7. Click the **Done** button to return to your message.

Search Email Messages

You can search through your messages to find specific topics or messages that contain specific content. To search your email messages, perform the following steps:

1. From the Inbox (click the **Inbox** icon if you are not there), click the **Find Message** link.

2. Enter the word or phrase you are searching for in the first text field.

3. Click your selection to search only the subjects of messages or entire messages.

4. Click your selection for those folders that you want Hotmail to search.

5. Click **Search**. A results page provides a list of those messages that are found to contain your search words.

Create an Email Address Book

You can create and save email addresses of the people you communicate with frequently in a Hotmail Address Book. To create (populate) your address book, perform the following steps:

1. Click **Addresses** in the Navigation window.
2. Click the **Create** link next to the Individuals Address area.
3. Enter a nickname and email address for the individual.
4. Click **OK**.

NOTE

You can add personal information such as phone number, address, and even date of birth to the file for any nickname.

NOTE

You can create addresses for individuals or for groups. When you want to create a Group, select a name for the group (such as CarPool—no spaces in the nickname), and then enter all the email addresses for people who are in the group. You mail to everyone in the group simply by selecting the Group name that you just created and then clicking Send.

Use the Address Book and Quicklist

The easiest way to use the address book is to click the nickname for the individual or group you want to mail to. The Compose screen appears with the name in the To: field. If you want to send a message to several people who are in your address book, perform the following steps:

1. From the Hotmail home page, click **Addresses**.
2. From the Addresses screen that appears, click **Quicklist**.
3. Click in the check box for **To:, CC:,** or **BCC:** next to the nickname that you want to send mail to.
4. Click the **Mail To** button.
5. Compose and send the message.

Search for Other Hotmailers in the Member Directory

Hotmail has millions of subscribers. Your friends or family members might have Hotmail accounts. You can access the Hotmail member directory from the Inbox, Compose, or the Addresses window. To find and search the member directory, perform the following steps:

1. From the Inbox, Compose, or Addresses screen, click the **Hotmail Member Directory** link. (It is located in the upper-right corner of the screen.)
2. Enter the first and last name of the person that you are looking for.
3. Select Anywhere in the World or select a specific country under Choose a Country.
4. Click **Search**.
5. The results page will list people who match your search.

TIP

A common name such as Bill Smith might offer lots of results. Entries are not case sensitive. If a member search generates more than 100 matches, you will need to narrow the search (by state or country).

Create an Email Signature File

You can create a signature file—your online signature—that you can quickly add to any email message that you compose. The contents of your signature file are added to the end of a message when you click the Add Signature link or check box that is on the Compose page. Following is an example of what you might choose for a signature file, when you want to provide a little more information about yourself:

Bill Eager (: Internet Expert (:

Eager@rmi.net * 1243 Main Street * Chicago, IL 70432

Phone: (312) 777-7777 Fax: (312) 888-8888

38

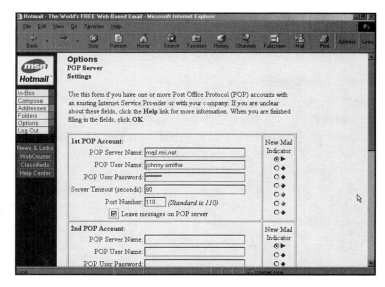

To create your email signature file, perform the following steps:

1. Click the **Options** button on the Navigation window.

2. Click the **Signature** link under Additional options.

3. Type your Signature message into the Signature text box.

4. Click **OK**.

Forward Email from Other Mail Accounts to Hotmail

If you have other email accounts, you can forward your mail from those accounts to your Hotmail account. (In fact, you can forward as many as four email accounts simultaneously to Hotmail.) This might be useful, say, if you go on vacation to a place where it is easier to retrieve mail from Hotmail. To set up this forwarding, perform the following steps:

1. Click **Options** in the Navigation window.

2. Click **POP Mail** under Mail Handling.

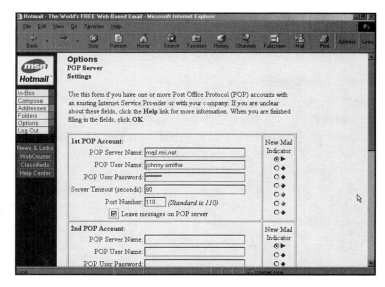

3. Enter the **POP Server Name**. The POP Server name is usually in the format mail.yourisp.com where yourisp is the name of your Internet service provider. You can try this, or ask your ISP what the POP mail server name is.

4. Enter the **POP User Name** (your username on that account).

5. Enter the **POP User Password** (the password you use to access email with your other account).

6. Select **server timeout** (the amount of time that Hotmail will wait to get a response from your ISP account). The 90-seconds default is usually fine, so you can leave this alone.

7. Select port number. The default of 110 is standard, so you can leave this alone. (If you are curious, the port number refers to a port on the mail server that enables you to access the mail.)

8. Check the leave messages on POP server check box if you want to leave all your mail messages on your other account. What this means is that you will be accessing a copy of the mail messages on Hotmail.

9. Click **OK**. Now when messages are received on your ISP account, they will be forwarded to Hotmail as well.

USING NETSCAPE MESSENGER

Netscape Messenger is the email program that comes built in with the Netscape Navigator software program. With this program, it's easy to move back and forth from the Web to email.

The upcoming subsections offer detailed instruction for performing tasks relating to Netscape Messenger as an email service.

Quick Tips

Function	Button	Keyboard Shortcut
Launch Messenger		Ctrl + 2
Address Book		Ctrl + ⬆Shift + 2
Search Messages		Ctrl + ⬆Shift + F
Retrieve Mail	Get Msg	Ctrl + T
New Message	New Msg	Ctrl + M
Reply to Message	Reply	Ctrl + R
Reply to All	Reply All	Ctrl + ⬆Shift + R
Forward Message	Forward	Ctrl + L

Launch Netscape Messenger

To launch Netscape Messenger, you must first start Netscape. Perform the following steps:

1. Start Netscape Navigator (either from Windows Programs or the taskbar).
2. Select **Communicator**, then **Messenger** (or Ctrl + 2).

Check and Read Email

To check for and read your messages in Netscape Messenger, perform the following steps:

1. Launch Netscape Messenger (see the previous section).
2. Click the Inbox folder.
3. Click the **Get Message** button ![Get Msg] on the toolbar.
4. Click the message that you want to read.
5. View the message in the Message window.

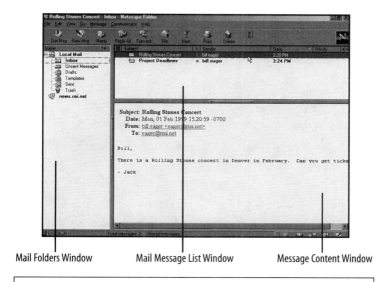

| Mail Folders Window | Mail Message List Window | Message Content Window |

TIP

To quickly sort your messages alphabetically, click the Subject bar that is at the top of all the messages.

Reply to or Forward a Message

To reply to a message you have received or to forward it, perform the following steps:

1. Highlight the message you want to reply to or forward by clicking on it one time.
2. Click **Reply** or **Forward** on the toolbar.
3. Type your message.
4. Click **Send**.

Save a Message

To save a message you have received, perform the following steps:

1. Open the email message you want to save (see the section "Check and Read Email").
2. Choose **File**, then **Save As File** (or Ctrl+S).
3. Type a filename.

4. Select the directory where you want the file to be saved.

5. Click **Save**. The message is saved as a text file in the specified directory.

Delete a Message

You can delete any message. Perform the following steps:

1. Highlight the message in the Message Inbox by clicking on it.

2. Press Del on your keyboard.

3. The message is moved to the Trash folder. At any time, you can open the Trash folder by double-clicking it. Then, again, delete (permanently this time) the message by clicking it and pressing the Del key on your keyboard.

Create Folders for Mail Messages

You can organize your email messages by filing them in folders. Netscape Messenger provides several default folders (see Table 9).

Table 9

Netscape Messenger Default Folders

Folder	Purpose
Inbox	Incoming mail
Unsent Messages	Messages not delivered
Drafts	Drafts of messages
Templates	Store message templates for future use
Sent	Delivered messages
Trash	Messages that you plan to delete

You can create as many additional folders as you desire to help identify and store mail—from Family or Business for example. To create a new message folder, perform the following steps:

1. From the main Netscape Messenger screen, choose **File**, then **New Folder**.

2. In the Name field type the name of this folder.

3. Click **OK**.

Organize Messages

Organizing your messages is easy. You organize them into folders—either the default folders provided by Netscape Messenger or the customized folders you create (see the previous section). To organize your messages, perform the following tasks:

1. Click a message in the Messenger Inbox to highlight it.

2. Drag the message to the folder where you want to move it.

Compose and Send Email

To create a new message and to send it, perform the following steps:

1. Click the **New Message** button on the toolbar to open the Composition window.

2. In the To: field, type the email address of the recipient. Or, click the **Address Book** to use a stored email address (see "Create an Email Address Book").

3. In the Subject: field, type the subject of this message.

4. In the message text area, type your message.

5. Click the **Send** button on the toolbar.

> **TIP**
>
> If you are going to regularly send a report or email with a standard format or table, you can save time by saving the message in the Template folder. Then, simply open the message, make any modifications, and send the new message.

Add an Attachment

One great aspect of email is that you can send people more than just words. You can attach files to your email messages. Appropriately referred to as attachments, these files can really be anything: digital photographs, word processing files, spreadsheets, sound files. The person whom you send the attachment to can then view, read, listen to, or use your file. To add an attachment to a message you are creating, perform the following steps:

1. Start a new message by clicking on the **New Message** button on the Messenger toolbar.

2. When you have finished composing your mail, click the **Attach** button on the mail composition toolbar and select **file** (you can also choose to attach a Web page).

3. Browse through your hard drive until you locate the file you want to attach. Double-click the file when you find it; the file is now attached to the mail message.

Create an Email Address Book

After you use email for a little while, you'll start to gather a large list of friends, family, and colleagues who have email addresses. Most email programs enable you to save a list of people with their email addresses in an electronic address book. Open this address book and you can quickly select one or more people to send your messages to. To create your address book, perform the following steps:

1. Choose **Communicator**, then **Address Book**.

2. On the Address Book window, click **New Card** on the toolbar.

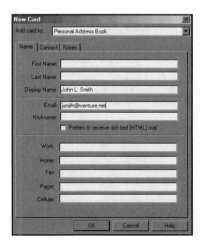

3. Type a first name, last name, email address, and nickname for the person. (The only required fields for an
   Address Book entry are display name and email; you can
   use the Address book to store other useful information
   about people.)

4. Click **OK**.

TIP

When you get an email message from someone, you can quickly
add them to your address book. Right-click the message, and then
select Add sender to address book.

Create a List for the Address Book

A list in your address book (see the previous section) is a
group of email addresses all stored as one name. To create
a list, perform the following steps:

1. Choose **Communicator**, then **Address Book**.

2. From the Address Book window, click the **New List**
   button.

3. Type the name of the list in the List Name field.

4. Type email addresses into the mailing list.

5. Click **OK** to create this list.

TIP

You can also simply drag names from your personal address book,
or results pages from a Netcenter Member Directory or Infospace
Directory search into the mailing list box and the names and
addresses will be added.

Import Addresses

You can import addresses into Messenger from other email
programs that you might have. Perform the following steps:

1. Open the Address Book (Ctrl+Shift+2) from the
   Messenger main window).

2. Select **File**, then **Import**.

3. Messenger displays available address books. Click one, and then click the **Next** button.

4. Select the mailboxes, and then click **Next**.

5. Select the address book and click **Finish**. All your addresses are copied into Messenger and are available from the Address Book.

Search for Email Addresses

You can search for the email addresses of people who have signed up with Netscape's Net Center Web site, are on the Infospace directory, or the VeriSign directory. These are all different email repositories available on the Web. From the Address Book Window you can search for email addresses by performing the following steps:

1. Open the Address Book (Ctrl+Shift+2 from the Messenger main window).

2. Click one of the folders labeled **Netscape Member Directory**, **Infospace Directory**, or **VeriSign Directory** (which appear on the left side of the window).

3. In the **Show Names Containing** field, type a person's name.

4. Click the **Search For** button.

5. Double-click any name in the results window to obtain more details.

USING OUTLOOK EXPRESS

Outlook Express is Microsoft's full-featured email client that is included with standard or full installations of Internet Explorer 4.0, Windows 98, and Office 97 and 2000. If you don't already have it, you can download Internet Explorer from the Microsoft Web site (`www.microsoft.com`) to get it.

The upcoming subsections offer detailed instruction for performing tasks relating to Outlook Express as an email service.

Quick Tips

Feature	Button	Keyboard Shortcut
Compose Message		Ctrl + N
Reply to Author		Ctrl + R
Forward Message		Ctrl + F
Spell check a Message		
Delete a Message		Ctrl + P
Send and Receive		Ctrl + M
Select All		Ctrl + A
Go to a Folder		Ctrl + Y
Print a Message		Ctrl + P

Launch Outlook Express

There are two ways to launch Outlook Express. Perform the following steps:

1. Click the Outlook Express icon on the Desktop.

   Or

2. Launch Internet Explorer.
3. Click **Mail** on the toolbar.
4. Choose **Read Mail**.

NOTE

If you are not online when you launch Outlook Express from the desktop, it will ask you to select one of your dial-up accounts, and then begin the login process.

Check and Read Email

To check for and read your messages in Outlook Express, perform the following steps:

1. From within Outlook Express, click **Inbox** on the list of folders at the left side of the screen.

USING OUTLOOK EXPRESS

2. Click the **Send and Receive** button 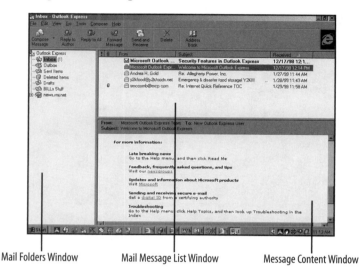 on the toolbar.

3. New messages appear in the messages window. Click once to view in the message window; double-click to open the message in a new window.

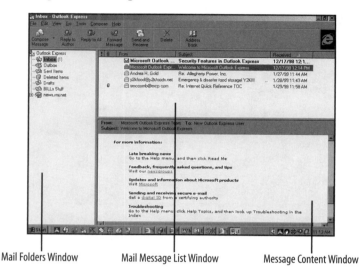

Mail Folders Window   Mail Message List Window   Message Content Window

Set Time for Checking Mail Messages

There are several settings you can establish with Outlook Express. One is the number of minutes Outlook Express will wait before checking for new mail. To establish this setting, perform the following steps:

1. From within Outlook Express, choose **Tools**, then **Options**.

2. On the General Tab, select **Check for New Messages Every....**

3. Enter the number of minutes that Outlook Express will wait before checking for new mail.

Reply to and Forward Messages

To reply to or to forward a message you have received, perform the following steps:

1. From within Outlook Express, click **Inbox** on the list of folders at the left side of the screen.

2. Highlight the message in the Inbox that you want to reply to or forward by clicking on it one time.

3. To reply, click the **Reply to Author** button ⬛ on the toolbar; to forward, click the **Forward Message** button ⬛.

4. Type an email address in the To: field (for forwarding).

5. Enter text (your message).

6. Click **Send**.

Save a Message

To save a message you have received, perform the following steps:

1. Open the email message you want to save (see the section "Check and Read Email").

2. Choose **File**, then **Save As**.

3. Type a filename.

4. Select the directory where you want the file to be saved.

5. Click **Save**. The message is saved as a text file in the specified directory.

Delete a Message

You can delete any message. Perform the following steps:

1. Highlight the message in the Message Inbox by clicking it.

2. Press **Delete** on your keyboard.

3. The message is moved to the Deleted Items folder. At any time, you can open the Deleted Items folder by double-clicking it. Then, again, delete (permanently this time) the message by clicking it and pressing the Delete key on your keyboard.

Create Folders for Mail Messages

Outlook provides you with the folders listed in Table 10.

Table 10

Outlook Express Folders

Outlook Mail Folder	Purpose
Inbox	Where new messages are received
Outbox	Temporarily holds outgoing messages until delivery
Sent Items	Stores copies of messages you send
Deleted Items	Stores messages you delete
Drafts	Store drafts of messages

You might, however, want to create several new folders to organize your messages—perhaps a folder for messages from work, one for messages from family, and so forth. To create an email folder, perform the following steps:

1. From within Outlook Express, choose **File**, then **Folder**, then **New**.
2. Type the name for the folder. Be certain that you are creating the new folder in Outlook Express (because you can also nestle folders inside other folders).
3. Click **OK**.

Organize Messages

Outlook makes it easy to organize your messages. After you've created the folders you want to serve as your filing system (see the previous section), you simply move your messages in and out of these folders as you please. To move a message, perform the following steps:

1. From within any folder (including the Inbox, of course), click the message that you want to move to another folder (holding the mouse down).
2. Holding the mouse down, drag the message to the folder you want to place it in.

TIP

Ctrl+A selects all messages. Or, you can hold down the Ctrl key and click multiple messages if you want to highlight and move several messages at one time.

Compose and Send Email

To create a new message and to send it, perform the following steps:

1. From within Outlook Express, click the Compose Message button on the toolbar.

2. Enter the email address of the recipient. Or click the **Address Book** button to use a stored email address (see "Create an Email Address Book").

3. Tab down to the Subject field and enter the subject for the message.

4. Tab down to the New Message Window area and enter the message.

5. Click the **Send** button to send the message.

TIP

Outlook offers some precreated messages that include graphics. Choose Compose, then New Message Using and select one of the Message Templates. For example, Balloon Party Invitation has pictures of balloons with Day, Time, and Place all ready for your text.

Add an Attachment

One great aspect of email is that you can send people more than just words. You can attach files to your email messages. Appropriately referred to as attachments, these files can really be anything: digital photographs, word processing files, spreadsheets, sound files. The person to whom you send the attachment can then view, read, listen to, or use your file. To add an attachment to a message you are creating, perform the following steps:

1. From within Outlook Express, click the Compose Message button on the toolbar.

2. From the New Message window, choose **Insert**, then **File Attachment**.

3. Locate the file on your hard drive.

4. Click **Attach**.

Add Links, HTML, and Images to Messages

You can include links to other Web sites (hyperlinks), and embed HTML code and images in your Outlook messages. Any person who uses Outlook (or other mail software that can read HTML) will see your links as hyperlinks in the message. Your HTML code will be viewed and your pictures will be embedded in the message. To add a hyperlink to a Web site or page, simply write the complete Web address in the format `www.espn.com`. HTML code enables you to select fonts, font colors, and sizes that your recipient will see. For example, if you wrote `<b>Hello</b>`, the word `Hello` would be in bold. If you do use HTML in your message, be sure that you start your HTML with the `<html>` tag and end the message with the `</html>` tag. To insert a picture into a message, perform the following steps:

1. Place your cursor in the New Message window (where you type text).

2. Choose **Insert**, then **Picture**.

3. Type the directory path for the picture or click Browse to locate picture files on your hard drive.

4. Click **Open**, then **OK** and the image will be placed in the message.

Create an Email Address Book

Your email address book is a convenient way to store the names and addresses of people you mail to frequently. To add someone to the Address Book, perform the following tasks:

1. From within Outlook Express, click **Address Book** on the Toolbar.

2. Click **New Contact** to add an individual to the address book.

3. Type First Name, Last Name, and Display Name in these fields.

4. Type their mail address in the Email address field.

5. Click **Add**, then **OK**.

> **NOTE**
>
> When you add someone to the address book, you can enter several email addresses for one individual (as many people have more than one today). However, you can select only one of these addresses as the default address. You can change the default at any time. If you want to set up several addresses for one person, you can also create several different profiles, such as bill eager1, bill eager2, and so on.

Import an Address Book from Other Programs

It is easy to import an address book from another email program into Outlook. So, whether you also use Netscape Navigator, Eudora, or another email program, you can quickly add this address book to Outlook. To import an address book, perform the following tasks:

1. From within Outlook Express, choose **File**, then **Import**, then **Address Book**.

2. Outlook shows a list of available address books. Click the name of the address book or file type you want to import, and then click **Import**.

> **TIP**
>
> If your address book is not on the Import list, you can first export it to either a text (CSV) file or an LDIF (LDAP Directory Interchange Format) file. Then import it into Outlook with one of these options.

Create a Signature File

You can create a signature file (your online signature) that you can quickly add to any email message you compose. The contents of your signature file are added to the end of a message. To create your email signature file, perform the following steps:

1. From within Outlook Express, choose **Tools**, then **Stationery**.

2. Click the **Signature** button on the **Mail** tab.

3. Type your signature (text) in the text box.

4. Click the **Add This Signature to All Outgoing Messages** box if you always want to use it.

5. Click **OK**.

Add a Signature to a Message

To add the signature file you've created (see the previous section) to an outgoing message, perform the following steps:

1. From within Outlook Express, click the **Compose Message** button on the toolbar.

2. After you have composed your message, select **Insert**, then **Signature**. You must create a signature before you can use it (see the previous section).

WEB-BASED EMAIL

With Web-based email, you go to a Web site and sign up for an email account and address. Then, you use the Web site to receive, compose, store, and organize your messages. The hottest Web-based email right now is Hotmail (see "Using Hotmail").

Why would you want to use a Web site to do this if you already have an email program? Well, for one thing you can receive and send email from anywhere in the world from the Web site! Normally, you would have to call long distance to your Internet service provider, and then log in to check email. Or you would have to first find, and then use a local phone number if you have a national Internet service such as Netcom or America Online. With Web-based email, you can walk into any cybercafé (a coffee-house that has Internet access), sit down, and check your messages in a few minutes. Many airports and hotels also have terminals where you can access the Web to check your email.

Table 11 shows a few Web sites that offer email accounts; most are completely free.

Table 11
Web-Based Email Accounts

Site	Address
Excite	www.excite.com
Eudora	www.eudoramail.com
Go	www.go.com
Hotmail	www.hotmail.com
Netscape	www.netscape.com
Snap	www.snap.com
Yahoo!	www.yahoo.com

NEWSGROUPS,
MESSAGE BOARDS,
AND MAILING LISTS

One of the great aspects of the Internet is that it represents a global party line. You can share your ideas, thoughts, questions, and concerns with millions of other people. And, you can tap into useful advice and interesting information. Newsgroups, message boards, and mailing lists offer almost unlimited resources where you can receive messages and participate in ongoing discussions with millions of other Net users. This section covers these three Internet services. Specifically, this section addresses the following main topic areas:

- Introduction to Newsgroups
- Newsgroup Names
- Using America Online for Newsgroups
- Using Deja News
- Using Netscape Communicator
- Using Outlook Express
- Yahoo! Message Boards
- Mailing Lists

INTRODUCTION TO NEWSGROUPS

Newsgroups (also known as Usenet) are a popular method for the exchange of ideas on a variety of topics. You can find a topic that you have an interest in, and then either read the ongoing discussion of other people from around the world, or join in the discussion yourself. Because these discussions take place with messages, they are not in real-time as is a chat session. But, in some ways, newsgroups are better than chat because the information is stored and you can find what you are looking for later.

Officially, newsgroups are known as Usenet (users network) newsgroups. Technically, Usenet uses the Internet to distribute messages (also called articles) on specific subjects. Newsgroups are categorized by subject, and the articles are added to specific newsgroups. For example, the newsgroup `rec.outdoors.fishing` contains articles about guess what? Fishing!

Are newsgroups popular? You bet! There are more than 24,000 different newsgroups. Every day, an estimated one million new messages (known as articles) are added to newsgroups. In fact, there are so many messages that most ISPs save messages on their computers for only two or three weeks.

If you only read other people's newsgroup messages, you are known as *a lurker*. Nothing is wrong with being a lurker if you find what you want. If you want to participate, you can send a message back to the newsgroup (in which case the entire world can read your message). This is referred to as *posting* your message. You can also send a mail message only to the author of a message that you find interesting. This can begin a nice two-way dialog.

There are some common terms used in the world of newsgroups that might be helpful:

- **Article** This is the message that you or other people add to a newsgroup.
- **Binary** A file that is attached to an article. Frequently pictures.
- **Flame** A nasty or inflammatory article that someone posts to a newsgroup.
- **FAQ (short for Frequently Asked Questions)** A list of common questions and answers about a newsgroup.
- **Lurker** Someone who reads messages but does not post any.
- **Newbie** A person who is just learning how to use newsgroups.
- **Newsgroup** A specific topic that has articles.
- **Post** To send your message to a newsgroup.
- **Shout** To type IN ALL CAPITAL LETTERS.
- **SPAM** To send the same message to many newsgroups (also to send an email to many people, usually selling something).
- **Subject** The subject of a newsgroup article.

- **Subscribe**   Join a newsgroup to quickly view articles.
- **Thread**   An ongoing discussion among people related to one original message.
- **Usenet**   The complete name for newsgroups—Usenet Newsgroups.

CAUTION

Sometimes it's easy to forget that Newsgroups and Message Boards are public places. Whatever you say can be seen by literally millions of people. For privacy and security, it's usually wise not to put your address or phone number on a message.

Following are a few newsgroups that offer helpful tips and information.

news.newusers.questions
A newsgroup that answers questions from new users.

news.announce.newusers
New users can find useful tips and information here.

news.answers
This newsgroup has lists of Frequently Asked Questions for different newsgroups.

NOTE

Your ISP (see Section I, "Kickstart") might not offer access to every single newsgroup because there are so many. Some newsgroups get hundreds of new messages every day while others seem to never have messages. Good ISPs provide access to thousands of newsgroups.

TIP

If you are new to newsgroups and want to try posting without being embarrassed, look for the newsgroup designed specifically for first-time users. It is alt.testing and *all* the messages say something such as "just a test." This is a good way to see how quickly your message is added to the group.

NEWSGROUP NAMES

Newsgroups are categorized to make it a little easier to find what you're looking for. A hierarchy is used in an effort to organize topics. There are seven main categories at the top of this hierarchy (see Table 12). Then, each of these top-level categories is broken down into subcategories. One example of the main categories is that of alt, representing alternative (which translates into lots of different topics). You can find the newsgroup's name `alt.music.tapes`, which is a newsgroup for people who like music—specifically tapes. Another example, `alt.tv.xena`, translates to alternative, television, *Xena* (a popular TV show).

Table 12

Newsgroup Top-Level Categories

Newsgroup Top Level	Topics
Alt	Alternative—hundreds of different topics
Comp	Computer-related
Misc	Miscellaneous topics
News	News
Rec	Recreational, sports, hobbies
Sci	Science-related
Soc	Social and societal topics
Talk	Area for talk and discussion

There are many other newsgroups that don't fit into these eight popular categories. Countries, states, and even companies have newsgroup hierarchies. For example, `es` is the top level for Spain; `co` is the top level for Colorado; and `microsoft` is for Microsoft newsgroups.

USING AMERICA ONLINE FOR NEWSGROUPS

America Online (AOL) offers a very convenient and intuitive interface for both finding and participating in newsgroups. Most newsgroups are available and AOL lets you view as many as 30 days' worth of messages.

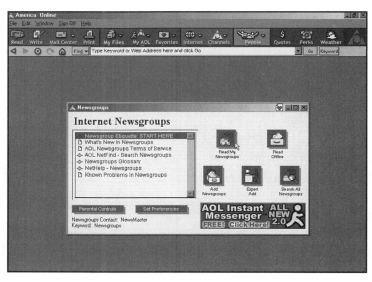

The upcoming subsections offer detailed instructions for performing tasks relating to AOL as a newsgroups service.

Search for and Subscribe to Newsgroups

There are two ways to use newsgroups. The first way is to simply search for a newsgroup and then retrieve current articles. The second way to use newsgroups is to subscribe to specific newsgroups. It costs nothing to subscribe; you simply use AOL to do this. The advantage to subscribing is that it saves you time. You quickly go to the newsgroup(s) that you subscribe to and receive current articles, so you eliminate the task of always finding the newsgroup. If you find that you don't like the articles on a newsgroup, you can always unsubscribe (see "Unsubscribe from a

Newsgroup"). To search for and subscribe to newsgroups, perform the following steps:

1. Launch AOL.
2. Choose **Internet** on the toolbar, then **Newsgroups**.
3. Click the **Search All Newsgroups** icon.
4. Type a keyword.

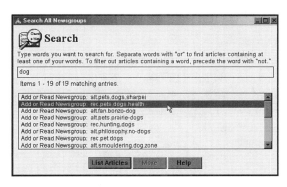

5. Click the **List Articles** button.
6. Double-click the name of a newsgroup in which you have an interest.
7. Click the **Subscribe to Newsgroup** link. Any newsgroup you subscribe to appears in the Read My Newsgroups section, which you access from the Newsgroups main page.

Locate and Subscribe to a Newsgroup by Name

In addition to finding newsgroups by using keywords, you can also locate and subscribe to them by starting with newsgroup domains and then locating newsgroups in specific categories. With America Online, it's worth trying both the search technique and this one. To locate and subscribe to a newsgroup by name, perform the following steps:

1. From within AOL, choose **Internet** on the toolbar, then **Newsgroups**.
2. Click the **Add Newsgroups** icon.

64

3. Double-click one of top-level newsgroup categories (such as rec or sci).

4. Now double-click one of the subcategories.

5. Highlight the newsgroup you want (such as **rec. aviation.military**) and click the **Subscribe** button. Any newsgroup you subscribe to appears in the Read My Newsgroups section, which you access from the Newsgroups main page.

Read a Newsgroup Message

Messages are the guts of newsgroups. They contain all the information and sometimes pictures that people share with one another. With AOL, you are only a couple of clicks away from reading the messages in any newsgroup that you've subscribed to. Perform the following steps:

1. From within AOL, choose **Internet** on the toolbar, then **Newsgroups**.

2. Click the **Read My Newsgroups** icon. This opens a list of *all* the newsgroups that you have subscribed to.

3. Double-click any newsgroup to get a list of unread messages.

4. Double-click an individual message to read it.

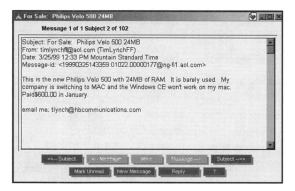

> **TIP**
>
> AOL lets you determine how many days' worth of messages you want to see. The maximum is 30 days. When you are in a newsgroup, click the Preferences button and change to the number of days you prefer.

Save a Newsgroup Message

To save a newsgroup message, perform the following steps:

1. Highlight or open the message (see the previous section) you want to save.

2. Choose **File**, then **Save** ($\boxed{\text{Ctrl}}$+$\boxed{\text{S}}$).

3. Type the filename, select the directory it should be saved to, and click **Save**. The message is then saved as a text file in whichever directory you select.

Reply to a Message: Reply to the Newsgroup

You can reply to the messages you read at a Newsgroup. You can reply either to the newsgroup as a whole or to the author of the message you're interested in. To reply to the newsgroup as a whole, perform the following steps:

1. Open the newsgroup message you want to reply to (see the previous section).

2. Click the **Reply** button.

3. The Post Response window opens. (By default, the message replies [posts] to the newsgroup.)

4. Type your message in the Reply window.

5. Click the **Send** button.

Reply to a Message: Reply to the Author

Again, you can reply to the messages you read at a Newsgroup. You can reply either to the newsgroup as a whole or to the author of the message you're interested in. To reply to the author, perform the following steps:

1. Open the newsgroup message you want to reply to (see "Read a Newsgroup Message").

2. Click the **Reply** button.

3. In the Post Response window, click the **Send via Email** check box (if you don't want the entire newsgroup to see your message, deselect the **Post to Newsgroup** check box).

4. Type your message in the **Reply** window.

5. Click the **Send** button.

Post a New Article

By posting an article (or message) to a newsgroup, you are participating in a global discussion. It is your chance to let other people read what you think. You might even be pleasantly surprised at the responses that people have to your information both on the newsgroup and in emails that you receive. To post an article, perform the following steps:

1. From within AOL, choose **Internet** on the toolbar, then **Newsgroups**.

2. Click the **Read My Newsgroups** icon. This opens a list of *all* the newsgroups that you have subscribed to.

3. Double-click any newsgroup to open a list of current messages.

4. At the bottom of this window, click the button labeled **New Message**.

5. Type a subject and your message (the address is already filled in). Click **Send**. Your message is on its way and is usually available at the newsgroup within a few hours.

Unsubscribe from a Newsgroup

If you've subscribed to a newsgroup (see "Search and Subscribe to Newsgroups") but no longer find it useful, you might want to unsubscribe. To do so, perform the following steps:

1. From within AOL, choose Internet on the toolbar, then Newsgroups.

2. Click the Read My Newsgroups icon. This opens a list of all the newsgroups that you have subscribed to.

3. Click the newsgroup you want to unsubscribe from, and click the **Remove** button at the bottom of this window.

USING DEJA NEWS

Deja News Web (**www.dejanews.com**) is the only Web-based newsgroup site that lets you read, search, participate in, and subscribe to some 80,000 discussion forums, including all the Usenet newsgroups. (A *discussion forum* is really a Web-based newsgroup where people share messages on a Web site; however, these messages do not become part of the standard Usenet newsgroup system.) You must register (it's free) to post and reply to messages and to have a personalized page where you can subscribe to newsgroups. Deja News offers more advantages than the traditional approach of using Outlook Express (see "Using Outlook Express") or Netscape Communicator (see "Using Netscape Communicator") to read newsgroup messages (the obvious advantage being an easy-to-use Web interface for searching and viewing messages). You can search through all the newsgroups simultaneously to find messages about specific topics, which you cannot do with Outlook or Communicator.

The upcoming subsections offer detailed instructions for performing tasks relating to Deja News as a newsgroups service.

Search Newsgroups

Every day, there are thousands and thousands of new articles posted on thousands of newsgroups. Finding one specific article about a subject that you are interested in can be a daunting challenge. Deja News helps out a little, as it has a search system in which you can type keywords and search for either individual articles or newsgroups that might contain your subject. To search newsgroups, perform the following steps:

1. From the Deja News Home page (**www.dejanews.com**), type a keyword in the Find field.

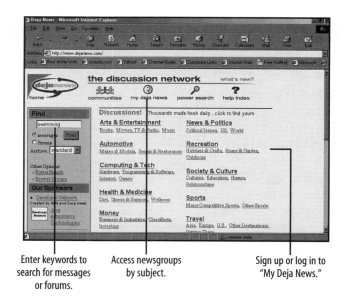

Enter keywords to search for messages or forums.

Access newsgroups by subject.

Sign up or log in to "My Deja News."

2. Choose **Messages** or **Forums** for your search (message search finds all messages with your keyword; forums finds any newsgroups that pertain to the subject).

3. Click Find.

Subscribe to a Newsgroup

There are two ways to use newsgroups. The first way is to simply search for a newsgroup and then retrieve current articles. The second way to use newsgroups is to subscribe to specific newsgroups. It costs nothing to subscribe; you simply use Deja News to do this. The advantage to subscribing is that it saves you time. You quickly go to the newsgroup(s) that you subscribe to and receive current articles, so you eliminate the task of always finding the newsgroup. If you find that you don't like the articles on a newsgroup, you can always unsubscribe. To subscribe to a newsgroup, perform the following steps:

1. Click My Deja News on the Deja News homepage (**www.dejanews.com**), and log in to My Deja News with your username and password (register first—it prompts you the first time you click My Deja News).

2. Click **Add/Remove Forum** subscriptions link.

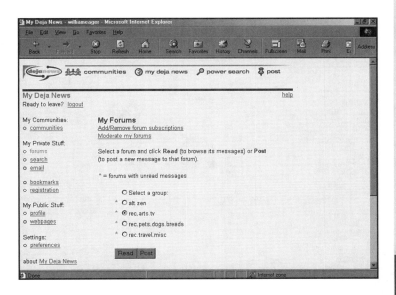

3. In the Add Forums field, type a keyword and click **Find Forums**.

4. Check the **Subscribe** box next to the newsgroup or forum that you want.

5. Click **Add.** You will now be able to quickly access this newsgroup and its articles the next time you visit My Deja News.

Read a Newsgroup Message

After you have subscribed to one or more newsgroups, you'll want to start reading the individual messages (articles) that are available. It's easy to do. Perform the following steps:

1. From the My Deja News home page (**www.dejanews.com**), click the option button next to the newsgroup you want to read (you must subscribe to a newsgroup before it will appear on this list).

2. Click **Read**.

3. Click the link (message titles) for the message you want to read.

4. Click the **Previous** and/or **Next** icon to move through messages.

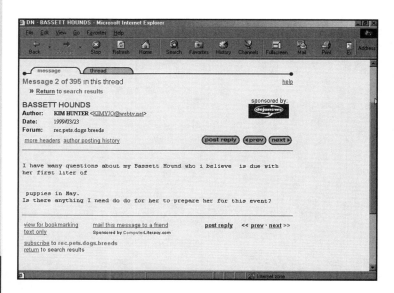

Search Messages in a Specific Newsgroup

Some individual newsgroups have thousands of messages. To help you save some time, Deja News makes it possible to keyword search individual newsgroups. Perform the following steps:

1. From My Deja News, go to a specific newsgroup (see previous section).

2. In the Search in This Forum field enter your keyword(s); click **GO**. You will receive a new page with a list of relevant messages that you can read.

Reply to a Message: Reply to the Newsgroup

You can reply to the messages you read at a Newsgroup. You can reply either to the newsgroup as a whole or to the author of the message you're interested in. To reply to the newsgroup as a whole, perform the following steps:

1. Open the message you want to reply to (see "Read a Newsgroup Message").

2. Click **Post Reply**.

3. Type your message in the Message box.

4. Click **Send**.

USING DEJA NEWS

NOTE

The first time that you reply to a message, Deja News asks you to confirm your email address.

Reply to a Message: Reply to the Author

You can reply to the messages you read at a Newsgroup. You can reply either to the newsgroup as a whole or to the author of the message you're interested in. To reply to the author, perform the following steps:

1. Open the message you want to reply to (see "Read a Newsgroup Message").

2. Click the email address that is beside the author's name.

3. Your email program will launch and you can send a reply message.

Explore Deja News Hot Topics

Deja News hot topics are newsgroups that get a lot of messages. Deja News organizes these in one convenient area for fast access. You might find `alt.coffee` for coffee lovers or `misc.invest.stocks` for stock advice. To find out what people are talking about (that is, to explore Deja News hot topics), perform the following steps:

1. From the Deja News home page (`www.dejanews.com`), scroll down to Top Forums.

2. Click a link to one of the top forums.

3. Click a link to a message you find interesting.

TIP

Deja News also organizes popular newsgroups into subject categories at the home page. Click a category, such as Health and Fitness, and access popular newsgroups in this category.

Netscape uses the same program for newsgroups as it does for email: Communicator. When you click the news server icon in Communicator (as opposed to the Inbox for mail), the toolbar changes to offer options specific to newsgroups.

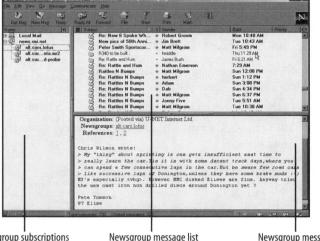

Newsgroup subscriptions   Newsgroup message list   Newsgroup message

Communicator makes it easy to locate and subscribe to newsgroups and to read and post messages. The upcoming subsections offer detailed instruction for performing tasks relating to Netscape Communicator as a newsgroup software program.

Quick Tips

Feature	*Button*	*Keyboard Shortcut*
New message		Ctrl + M
Reply to message		Ctrl + R
Reply to all		Ctrl + ⬆Shift + R
Forward message		Ctrl + F
Search messages		Ctrl + ⬆Shift + F

Search and Subscribe to Newsgroups

There are two ways to use newsgroups. The first way is to simply search for a newsgroup and then retrieve current articles. The second way to use newsgroups is to subscribe to specific newsgroups. It costs nothing to subscribe; you simply use Netscape Communicator to do this. The advantage to subscribing is that it saves you time. You quickly go to the newsgroup(s) that you subscribe to and receive current articles, so you eliminate the task of always finding the newsgroup. If you find that you don't like the articles on a newsgroup, you can always unsubscribe (see "Unsubscribe from a Newsgroup"). To search and subscribe to newsgroups, perform the following steps:

1. Launch Netscape Navigator.
2. Choose **Communicator**, then **Newsgroups**.
3. Choose **File**, then **Subscribe**.
4. Click the **Search** tab in the Subscribe to Newsgroups window.

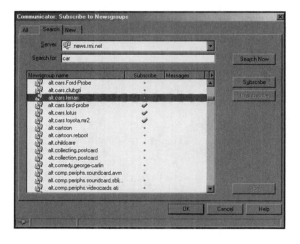

5. Type a keyword in the Search For field.
6. Click **Search Now**.
7. Click the names of any newsgroups you want to join.

8. Click **OK**. After you subscribe to a newsgroup, the name of the newsgroup appears in the left window of Communicator just below the news service. Just click it and you have instant access to messages in that newsgroup.

NOTE

The first time you open the Subscribe to Newsgroups window, Communicator downloads the list of *all* the available newsgroups from your ISP's news server. This can take a few minutes. The Subscribe to Communicator window shows all the top-level news-groups as folders. Click a folder to open the newsgroups in that category.

Read a Newsgroup Message

Messages are the guts of newsgroups. They contain all the information and sometimes pictures that people share with one another. Communicator's main window lets you simul-taneously view newsgroups, message subjects, and individual messages. Perform the following steps:

1. At the Communicator main window, double-click the name of the news server (such as `news.rmi.net`). This opens a list of newsgroups that you have subscribed to (see the previous section).

2. Click a newsgroup name (articles appear in the Message window).

3. Click an article to read it, or double-click an article to open it in a new window.

4. To view the next article in the thread, click the **Next** button on the toolbar.

NOTE

If an article has a small plus sign to the left of it, this means there is a discussion on the topic. Double-click the plus sign to see other articles.

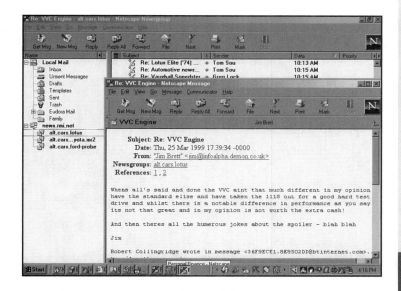

TIP

On top of the message window, you will see headers for the message subject, whom the message is from, and the date the message was sent. Click any of these to change the way the messages are sorted and displayed.

Save a Newsgroup Message

To save a newsgroup message, perform the following steps:

1. Highlight or open the message (see the previous section) you want to save.

2. Choose File, then Save As, then File.

3. Type your filename and click Save. The message is saved as a text file in whatever directory you select.

Reply to a Message: Reply to the Newsgroup

You can reply to the messages you read at a Newsgroup. You can reply either to the newsgroup as a whole or to the author of the message you're interested in. To reply to the newsgroup as a whole, perform the following steps:

1. Open the newsgroup message you want to reply to
   (see "Read a Newsgroup Message").
2. Click the **Reply** button ⬛ on the toolbar.
3. Add your text to the existing message.
4. Click **Send**.

Reply to a Message: Reply to the Author

You can reply to the messages you read at a Newsgroup. You
can reply either to the newsgroup as a whole or to the
author of the message you're interested in. To reply to
the newsgroup as a whole, perform the following steps:

1. Open the newsgroup message you want to reply to
   (see "Read a Newsgroup Message").
2. Choose **Message**, then **Reply**, then **Sender Only**.
3. Type your subject and message.
4. Click **Send**.

Post a New Article

By posting an article (or message) to a newsgroup, you are
participating in a global discussion. It is your chance to let
other people read what you think. You might even be
pleasantly surprised at the responses that people have to
your information both on the newsgroup and in emails that
you receive. To post an article, perform the following steps:

1. Choose the newsgroup you want to post to by clicking
   the name of the newsgroup in Communicator's main
   window (the newsgroups that you've subscribed to are
   listed under the name of the news server).
2. Click the **New Message** button ⬛ on the toolbar.
3. Type your subject and message.
4. Click **Send**. Your message is now on its way to the
   newsgroup. It usually takes several hours before your
   message shows up on all the news servers in the world.

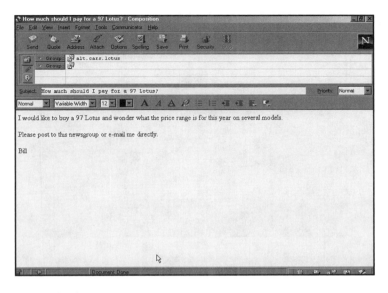

Unsubscribe from a Newsgroup

If you've subscribed to a newsgroup (see "Search and Subscribe to Newsgroups") but no longer find it useful, you might want to unsubscribe. To do so, perform the following steps:

1. Choose the newsgroup you want to unsubscribe from by clicking the name of the newsgroup in Communicator's main window (the newsgroups that you've subscribed to are listed under the name of the news server).

2. Choose **Edit**, then **Unsubscribe** or simply press the Delete key on your keyboard.

3. Communicator asks you whether you are sure you want to unsubscribe; click **OK**.

USING OUTLOOK EXPRESS

Outlook Express (the same program that is the email software that works with Internet Explorer) is the Microsoft program for newsgroups. You get to Outlook Express for newsgroups from Internet Explorer by clicking the Mail button on the toolbar and then choosing Read News.

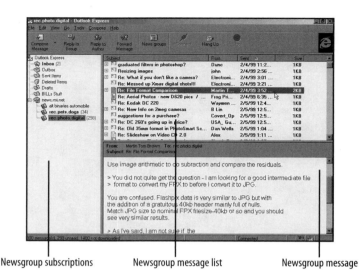

Newsgroup subscriptions   Newsgroup message list   Newsgroup message

The upcoming subsections offer detailed instructions for performing tasks relating to Outlook Express as a newsgroups service.

Quick Tips		
Feature	*Button*	*Keyboard Shortcut*
Open message		Ctrl + O
Compose a message		Ctrl + N
Reply to newsgroup		Ctrl + G
Reply to author		Ctrl + R
Forward a message		Ctrl + F
Download all		Ctrl + Shift + M

Search and Subscribe to Newsgroups

There are two ways to use newsgroups. The first way is to simply search for a newsgroup and then retrieve current articles. The second way to use newsgroups is to subscribe to specific newsgroups. It costs nothing to subscribe; you simply use Outlook Express to do this. The advantage to subscribing is that it saves you time. You quickly go to the

newsgroup(s) that you subscribe to and receive current articles, so you eliminate the task of always finding the newsgroup. If you find that you don't like the articles on a
newsgroup, you can always unsubscribe (see "Unsubscribe
from a Newsgroup"). To search and subscribe to newsgroups,
perform the following steps:

1. Launch Outlook Express (from within Internet
   Explorer, click the **Mail** button on the toolbar and then
   choose **Read News**).
2. Click the **News Groups** button ▣ on the toolbar.
3. If this is your first time with the newsgroups, click
   Reset List to get the most current list of newsgroups.
4. In the field `Display Newsgroups Which Contain`, type a
   subject that you would like to find a newsgroup (for
   example, pets or medicine).
5. Click the name of the newsgroup(s) you want.
6. Click **Subscribe**.

TIP

When you subscribe to a newsgroup, Outlook keeps that newsgroup listed in the Newsgroup subscription list for easy access. If,
however, you just want to try a newsgroup, instead of clicking
Subscribe in the Newsgroup display window, simply click Go To.

Read a Newsgroup Message

Messages are the guts of newsgroups. They contain all the
information and sometimes pictures that people share with
one another. Outlook's main window lets you simultaneously view newsgroups, message subjects, and individual
messages. To read a newsgroup message, perform the
following steps:

1. At the Outlook Express main window, double-click the
   name of the news server (for example, **news.rmi.net**).
   This opens a list of the newsgroups that you have
   subscribed to (see the previous section).
2. Click any specific newsgroup.

3. The current messages for this Newsgroup appear in the upper-right window.

4. Click once on any message to read the message in the window at the bottom of the screen, or double-click the message to open it in a new read message window.

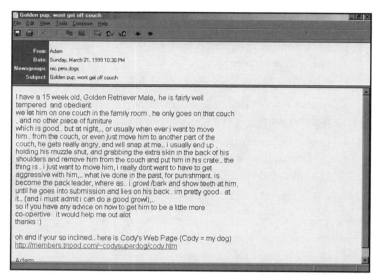

NOTE

If you see a plus sign to the left of the Subject, it means that several other people have already joined in a discussion about the topic. Click the plus sign to see all the messages related to the current subject.

TIP

On top of the message window, you will see headers for the message subject, whom the message is from, and the date the message was sent. Click any of these to change the way the messages are sorted and displayed.

Save a Newsgroup Message

To save a newsgroup message, perform the following steps:

1. Highlight the message (see the previous section) you want to save.

2. Choose **File**, then **Save As**.

3. Type a filename, choose the directory in which you want to place this file, and click **Save** (the file is saved as a text file).

Reply to a Message: Reply to the Newsgroup

You can reply to the messages you read at a Newsgroup. You can reply either to the newsgroup as a whole or to the author of the message you're interested in. To reply to the newsgroup as a whole, perform the following steps:

1. Highlight the message you want to reply to (see "Read a Newsgroup Message").

2. Click the **Reply to Group** button on the toolbar.

3. Type your message.

4. Click **Post** to post your message to the newsgroup.

NOTE

When you post a message to a newsgroup, it might not appear for several hours, possibly even a day, as your message is routed to all the newsgroup servers on the Internet.

Reply to a Message: Reply to the Author

You can reply to the messages you read at a Newsgroup. You can reply either to the newsgroup as a whole or to the author of the message you're interested in. To reply to the author, perform the following steps:

1. Highlight the message you want to reply to (see "Read a Newsgroup Message").

2. Click the **Reply to Author** button on the toolbar.

3. Type your message.

4. Click **Send** to send the message.

Post a New Article

By posting an article (or message) to a newsgroup, you are participating in a global discussion. It is your chance to let other people read what you think. You might even be pleasantly surprised at the responses that people have to your information both on the newsgroup and in emails that you receive. To post an article, perform the following steps:

1. Choose the newsgroup you want to post to by clicking the name of the newsgroup in Outlook Express (the newsgroups that you've subscribed to are listed under the name of the news server).

2. Click the **Compose Message** button on the toolbar.

3. Type your subject and the message (the address is already filled in).

4. Click **Send**. Your message is now on its way to the newsgroup. It usually takes several hours before your message shows up on all the news servers in the world.

Unsubscribe from a Newsgroup

If you've subscribed to a newsgroup (see "Search and Subscribe to Newsgroups") but no longer find it useful, you might want to unsubscribe. To do so, perform the following steps:

1. Choose the newsgroup you want to unsubscribe from by clicking the name of the newsgroup in Outlook Express (the newsgroups that you've subscribed to are listed under the name of the news server).

2. Choose **Tools**, then **Unsubscribe** from this newsgroup.

3. Outlook Express asks you whether you are sure you want to unsubscribe; click **Yes**.

YAHOO! MESSAGE BOARDS

Yahoo! is one of the most popular Web sites on the Net. Yahoo! started as a search engine and directory where you could find other Web sites. Today, the site offers much more, including message boards. Indeed, Yahoo! members have created hundreds and hundreds of message boards. These message boards are very similar to newsgroups— except that only members of Yahoo! are the participants.

The upcoming subsections offer detailed instructions for performing tasks relating to Yahoo! Message Boards.

Access Yahoo! Message Boards

To get to the Yahoo! Message Boards, perform the following steps:

1. While in your browser, go to `http://messages.yahoo.com`.
2. Click a link to one of the Message Board categories (such as **Health**).
3. Click a link to a subcategory (such as **Medicine**).
4. If necessary, click another subcategory, until you get a list of messages.

Search Yahoo! Message Boards

You can also perform searches with Yahoo! Message Boards. To do so, perform the following steps:

1. At the message board home page (`http://messages.yahoo.com`), type a keyword (such as `pets`).

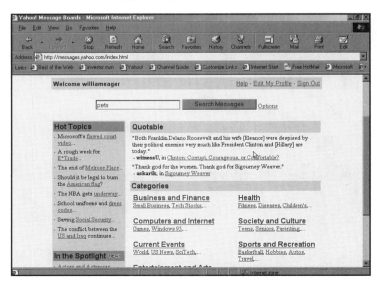

2. Click **Search Messages**.

3. You receive a list of both message boards and messages; click a message board link to go to the board, or a message to view the message.

TIP

The Yahoo! message boards about stocks are extremely popular. In the keyword field, type a stock symbol (for example, INTC for Intel) and search for the Intel message board.

Read a Yahoo! Message Board Message

To read a message you've located (see either of the previous two sections), perform the following steps:

1. Click a link to any message (see either of the previous two sections).

2. The message opens in a new page.

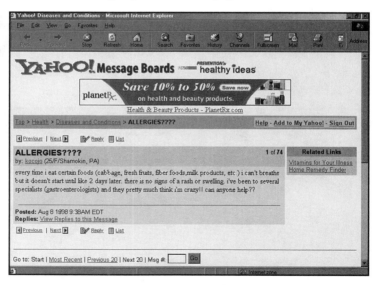

Yahoo! puts an easy-to-use Web interface on its message boards.

> **NOTE**
>
> Yahoo! always organizes messages by date with the most recent messages at the top of a page.

Reply to a Yahoo! Message Board Message

To reply to a message you've located (see "Access Yahoo! Message Boards" or "Search Yahoo! Message Boards"), perform the following steps:

1. Open the message you want to reply to (see "Access Yahoo! Message Boards" or "Search Yahoo! Message Boards").
2. Click the **Reply** icon at the top of the message.
3. On the Compose message page, type a subject.
4. Type your message.
5. Click **Post Message** (or Preview Before Posting).

MAILING LISTS

Do you like to get email? If so, then a mailing list is just the thing for you. Mailing lists enable people who share a common interest to exchange their ideas via electronic mail. Every member of a mailing list receives email copies of the messages that go to the list. There are more than 90,000 mailing lists that range in subject from antiques to marketing to scuba diving.

Some mailing lists are moderated and some are unmoderated. With a moderated mailing list, all the messages are reviewed prior to being sent out to the group. With an unmoderated list, all the messages are automatically redistributed.

Every mailing list has two email addresses. One is the address that you use to both subscribe and unsubscribe from the list. This is known as the administrative address. The second is the address where you send messages that are then re-sent to the members of the list. This is known as the list address. It is very important that you don't send your request to subscribe to the list address, because you will be sending it to all the list members—and they can't help you.

To get started with mailing lists, you need to know how to subscribe (and unsubscribe), and how you can find mailing lists that have topics you find interesting. The next two sections will help you.

Subscribe to and Unsubscribe from a Mailing List

Mailing lists are either maintained manually or automatically. Automated mailing lists are most popular. With an automated mailing list, a computer actually takes your information and adds you to the list. There are several different types of mail-server software programs that do this work. You will recognize the name of the software in the administrative address for automated lists. These include:

- Listproc
- LISTSERV
- Mailserve
- Majordomo

To subscribe to one of the automated mailing lists, send a message to the administrative address. Don't put any subject on your message and the message itself should be

SUBSCRIBE *listname your-name*

To unsubscribe send:

UNSUBSCRIBE *listname*

The computer software actually reads these messages and adds you to the mailing list. Your message is known as a list command because you are sending a command to the computer. Here is an example of an automated mailing list for the musical band Talking Heads.

List name: talking-heads

List Address: `talking-heads@ukans.edu`
Administrative Address: `listproc@raven.cc.ukans.edu`

List Type: listproc

Description: The Talking Heads mailing list, `talking-heads@ukans.edu`, was created so that fans of the musical group Talking Heads (and of its individual members David Byrne, Tina Weymouth, Chris Frantz, and Jerry Harrison) could discuss and exchange information about this extraordinary musical phenomenon. The list is public and unmoderated.

Subscribe: send list command to `listproc@raven.cc.ukans.edu`

So, your message to join this mailing list is:

subscribe talking-heads *YOUR FULL NAME*

TIP

Two other commands that you can email (in your message) to the administrative list include info and help. The computer mails you instructions about the mailing list.

With a manual mailing list, a person actually reviews your request and adds you to the list. When you send a subscription request to a manual mailing list, your message must include

- A short sentence that says, "Please add me to the ___ list"
- Your real name
- Your email address

To unsubscribe to a manual mailing list send another message that says you want to be taken off the list.

NOTE

A large percentage of mailing lists now have Web pages where you can subscribe, unsubscribe, and read messages. It makes it a lot easier because there are onscreen forms where you type your name and email address.

88

Find Mailing Lists

There are several good Web sites that offer keyword searching of thousands of mailing lists.

Liszt

Web address: `www.liszt.com`
Search by keyword or category through more than 90,000 mailing lists. Includes information about the lists and directions on subscribing and unsubscribing. Links to Web pages for mailing lists.

One List

Web address: `www.onelist.com`
ONElist is a free Web site that lets you access a variety of email communities. You can start and manage a new email community, subscribe to existing communities, and view archives of old messages.

Search Engines

Go to one of the search engines and type `mailing list`. You will get a variety of Web sites that provide access to mailing lists.

MAILING LISTS

TIP

Some mailing lists are very active, which means that you can get dozens of messages every day. Initially, try subscribing to only one or two mailing lists and wait to see how many messages you get. Your email box can fill up rather quickly, and what seems like a great resource can become a source of junk mail.

SECTION IV

ONLINE COMMUNICATION

Email and newsgroups are terrific tools for sharing information (see the previous two sections). But there is something special about communication that takes place in real-time. The Internet offers several methods by which you can carry on live conversations with other people. Chat is probably the most popular form of real-time communication on the Internet. With chat, you use your keyboard to type in messages that are shared instantaneously with one person or a group of people. Chatting offers a fun opportunity to have a spontaneous dialog with a friend or relative from a distance over the Internet.

Connect a microphone, speakers, and a small video camera to your PC and you can have a telephone conversation, or a videoconference. You can also use collaboration software to share images, files, or even software applications. Another option for online communications is *unified messaging*, where you connect your voicemail, fax, email, or even pager to one system for easy access.

Each of these online communication possibilities is covered in this section. Specifically, this section addresses the following main topic areas:

- Introduction to Chat
- Using America Online Chat
- Using Talk City Chat
- Using Yahoo! Chat
- Internet Telephony and Videoconferencing
- Unified Messaging
- Using Microsoft NetMeeting

INTRODUCTION TO CHAT

Chat on the Internet is very similar to what it is in our everyday life. We talk with friends, family, even strangers. The biggest difference with Internet chat is that you don't use your voice, only your keyboard. You type in your thoughts, and your words are viewed instantly by other people on their computer screens. They see what you type, and you see what they type. Of course, with the Internet you can chat with one, two, or even hundreds of other people simultaneously. Technically, you visit a Web site or an online service (such as America Online) and enter an area devoted to chat. Most chat areas are categorized by topic, so you are chatting with other people who share a common interest.

First-time chat users might be a little overwhelmed by what they see on the computer screen. Sometimes a chat session has 30 or more people talking. Some people are talking to the group, and others are essentially having private conversations that the group can view. So, it is a little confusing until you jump in.

Online services such as America Online and Web sites such as Yahoo! offer scheduled chats. These are chats where a famous person or an authority on a subject chats at a specific time. Sometimes these chats are moderated and the moderator filters questions that go to the speaker. After the premiere of his symphony *Stone Soup*, Paul McCartney had an online chat with his fans.

Following are some common chat definitions to keep in mind:

- **Chat room**   A place where people chat, usually about a specific topic.
- **Chat window**   The onscreen window where chat messages are seen.
- **Instant message**   A private message that one chatter sends to another.
- **Moderated chat**   A chat where questions are filtered before being answered.
- **Private chat**   A one-on-one chat.
- **Profile**   The publicly available information that describes a user.
- **Scheduled chat**   A chat that occurs at a specific time.
- **Screen name**   The identification or name that a person uses when chatting.

92

You will discover that an increasing number of Web sites offer chat. Usually you have to become a member of the Web site, although some let you chat as a guest. The only challenge with Web-based chat is that you have to locate a site where other people are actually online. If there's no one there, it gets boring chatting with yourself. Talk City and Yahoo! (see later in this section) have chatters 24 hours a day. Table 13 offers a few other sites you can try.

Table 13
Web-Based Chat Sites

Chat Site	Web Address
Absolute Chat	www.absolutechat.com
Chat Zone	www.chat-zone.com
Cool Chat	www.coolchat.com
Digital Chat Net	www.digitalchat.net
Free Town	www.freetown.com
Lycos Chat	chat.lycoschat.com
Omni Chat	www.4-lane.com
Talk City	www.talkcity.com
Web America	www.webamerica.com
WWW.Chatting.Com	www.chatting.com
Yahoo! Chat	chat.yahoo.com

USING AMERICA ONLINE CHAT

America Online does chat very well. When you've got 16 million members, you have a lot of online communication. You can jump into a free-for-all lobby chat in a matter of seconds, locate a chat about a specific subject such as the arts or sports, or create your own chat session that is either available to all other AOL members, or only those that you want to invite (a private chat room).

The upcoming subsections offer detailed instructions for performing tasks relating to AOL as a chat service.

Getting into an AOL Chat

When you jump into a chat, the AOL chat screen appears. In addition to the chat window, you also see the list of screen names for people who are chatting and the chat text field in which you type your messages.

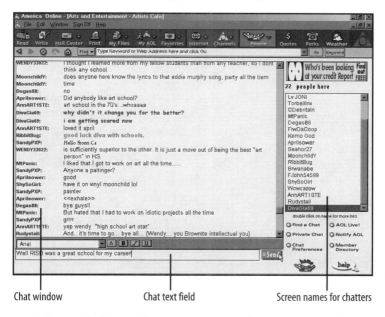

Chat window   Chat text field   Screen names for chatters

America Online makes it easy to use chat, with a window where you can see the chat conversation as well as other users.

Several other buttons are located on this screen. The following list indicates what they do:

- **Find a Chat**   Browse or search for specific chats by topic.
- **AOL Live!**   Find out when famous people will chat live.
- **Private Chat**   Enter or create a private chat room for your friends.
- **Notify AOL**   Report chat violations to AOL.

USING AMERICA ONLINE CHAT

- **Chat Preferences** Turn sounds on or off, line spacing, and other chat attributes.
- **Member Directory** Locate other AOL members to chat with, or read profiles of chatters.

The following steps get you into a Town Square lobby chat. This is a chat that is occurring the moment you enter. The reason you start here with AOL is because you instantly enter a live chat room and can start chatting immediately if you want to. AOL wisely limits the number of chatters in a chat room to 25 people. At any one time, there might be hundreds of these lobbies in use. The lobbies are randomly generated chats that simply place chatters into them. These chats are fun because you never know whom you will meet. This approach is a great way to start with chat because you can always find people in the Town Square chat rooms. The only downside is that people might be chatting about topics that you do not find interesting. It is not difficult to enter other chat rooms. Perform the following steps:

1. From within AOL, click the **People** button on the toolbar, then click **Chat Now**.
2. Type your message in the chat message field.
3. Click **Send** to add your message to the chat.

NOTE

Just above the chat text field you have options to change the way your messages appear onscreen. You can change the font, the color of your text, or add bold, italic, or underlined text.

Locate Chats by Subject

Wanting to find other people who are chatting about a topic that you find interesting is certainly not uncommon. That topic might be camping, basketball, country music, or politics. AOL helps you locate chat topics (such as Entertainment) and chat rooms (such as Fictional Books) that you can participate in. Other chat topics include countries such as Japan, the UK, or Canada where you can enter rooms where people are discussing topics about those countries (and usually you find people from those countries in the chat rooms). To locate chats by subject, perform the following steps:

1. From within AOL, click the **People** button on the toolbar, then **Find a Chat**.

2. Click and highlight a subject category (such as Life, News, Romance). Note that this Find a Chat screen also has a button to enter private chats.

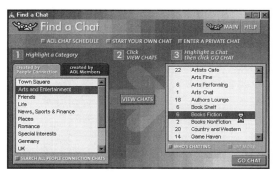

Search for chat rooms by topic or by geographic location.

3. Click **View Chats** to see a list of the chats that are going on now.

4. Click and highlight a specific chat that you find interesting.

5. Click **Go Chat**. The AOL chat room now opens and you are in the chat room for that topic.

Create a Public or Private Chat

AOL lets you create your own chat room and session. You can create a Member chat that will be listed for other AOL members to join (it is listed in the chat topics) or a Private Chat where only people that know the name of your chat room can join. To create a chat, perform the following steps:

1. From within AOL, click the **People** button on the toolbar, then **Start Your Own Chat**.

2. Choose either a **Member Chat** or a **Private Chat**.

3. Type the name for your chat room.

4. Click **Go Chat**. Your chat room is created and you automatically enter it. If it is public, then you need to wait for people to join your room. If it is private, you need to invite someone else to enter your room. That's because the chat room is not publicly listed and your friends need to know the name to find it. Other users access your private chat room by clicking the **Enter a Private Chat** button from the **Find a Chat** screen described in the previous section, "Locate Chats by Subject."

Send an Instant Message

An Instant Message allows you to send a private message to one other person within a chat session. The message appears only on their PC screen, and, if they want, they can send you one. Then, you have the option of either continuing the private conversation with these messages, or you can create and jump into a private chat (see the previous section). If you don't create a private chat, then other members in the current chat room can continue to send you messages. Sometimes people carry on private conversations with multiple parties simultaneously. To send an instant message, perform the following steps:

1. From within a chat session (see "Chat with AOL"), double-click someone's screen name.

2. Click **Send Message**.

3. Type your message.

4. Click **Send**.

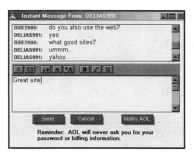

Create a New Screen Name

Your screen name is the name that other chatters see when you are in a chat room. If you want a little more privacy, or you want to create a screen name specifically for a chat area, you can create a second screen name. After you create a new screen name, it does not become effective until the next time you launch and sign on to AOL, and choose the new screen name. At the AOL sign in screen, you see a drop-down menu called Select Screen Name and you can pick the name you want. To create a new screen name, perform the following steps:

1. From within AOL, click the **My AOL** button on the toolbar and choose **Screen Names**.

2. Double-click **Create a Screen Name**.

3. Type a new screen name (you might have to be patient as someone else might have already selected your name).

4. Click the **Create a Screen Name** button.

Create (or Change) Your Profile

Every participant in a chat session has the opportunity to have a profile (they are not required). The concept of the profile is great. You can let other people know your areas of interest, the region of the world you live in, and so forth. To create (or change) your profile, perform the following steps:

1. From within AOL, click the **My AOL** button on the toolbar, then choose **My Member Profile**.

2. Formulate your profile as desired.

Access Another Chatter's Profile

Every participant in a chat session has a profile (if they so desire). A person's profile expresses his or her interests, locale, and so forth. To access someone's profile, perform the following steps:

1. From within a chat session, double-click someone's screen name (see "Getting into an AOL Chat").

2. Click **Get Profile**, and you see a screen that shows the profile that the chatter has created for himself.

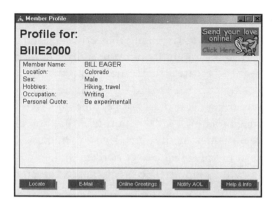

USING TALK CITY CHAT

Talk City is a popular Web site. The entire focus of Talk City is to build online communities of people that share common interests. It has more than one million members, so you'll find big communities and chat that occurs 24 hours a day on a variety of subjects. Chat is actually only one aspect of Talk City. You can build your own Web page, participate in bulletin boards, and visit online communities where people that share interests can exchange ideas.

Chat is easy and fun to use through Talk City. You can find a subject of interest and be chatting in less than one minute.

The upcoming subsections offer detailed instructions for performing tasks relating to Talk City as a chat service.

Find and Join a Chat

To get started chatting, you want to locate a community that shares your interests so that you can chat about topics you like. To find and join a chat, perform the following steps:

1. From within your browser, go to the Talk City home page at **www.talkcity.com**.

2. Click one of the home page links to a general community (such as auto, business, college, kids, family).

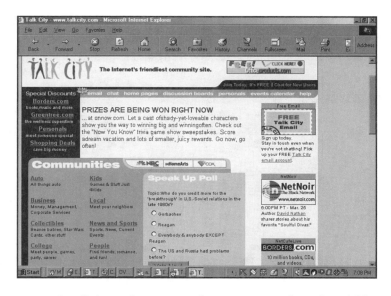

3. Scroll down the page until you come to a list of available chats.

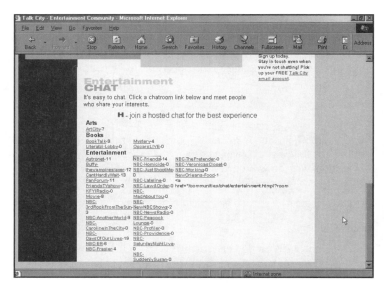

4. From the list of chat topics and the number of current chatters, select a chat room that you'd like to participate in by clicking it.

5. Talk City now opens a page where you log in to the system. At the login page, log in either as a member (with your name and password) or as a guest (create a nickname and use your email address).

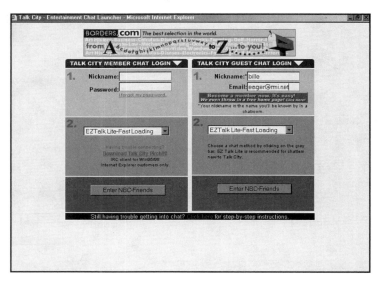

6. Enter the chat room by clicking the **Enter** button at the bottom of the page. This opens a new window with the current chat.

TIP

If a chat room has too many participants (more than 30), it can be difficult to follow the conversation. On the other hand, if you join a chat room with only three or four people, the conversation could be slow, or even nonexistent.

Chat at Talk City

The chat window is very intuitive. You'll find two windows. The left window contains a list of all the people who are in the chat room. The right window is the chat session, and you will find a field there for entering your chat. To chat at Talk City, perform the following steps:

1. From within a chat room (see the previous section), type your message in the chat field.

2. Press ⏎Enter on your keyboard.

3. Your message appears in the chat window.

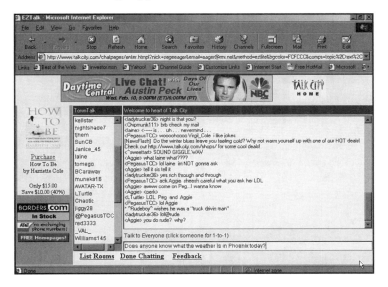

Establish One-on-One Chat

Sometimes you discover one person in a chat room with whom you would like to have a private conversation. To create a one-on-one chat, perform the following steps:

1. From within a chat session (see "Find and Join a Chat"), click (highlight) a user's name (names are in the left pane).

2. Type your message and press ⏎Enter on your keyboard. Your private message goes to this person.

3. To return to group chatting, click the top of the chat user's window (a blank user).

Jump to Other Rooms

At any time, you can find hundreds of chat rooms on Talk City, and you can jump from one to another quickly. To jump from your current chat room to another, perform the following steps:

1. From within a chat session (see "Find and Join a Chat"), click the **List Rooms** link at the bottom of the chat window.

2. From the list that appears, click a new chat group to participate in. You then enter that chat.

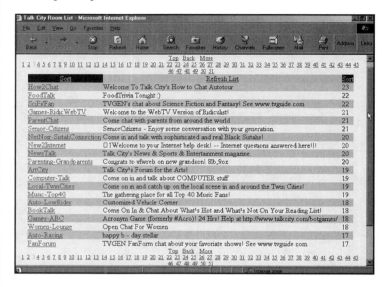

USING YAHOO! CHAT

Yahoo! is one of the most popular Web sites on the Internet. In addition to being a well-known site for locating other Web sites, Yahoo! has several chat features. Yahoo! offers regular moderated chat sessions in which you get an opportunity to chat with well-known people. For example, *NYPD Blue* star Sharon Lawrence and author Deepak Chopra were both chatting with Yahoo! members on Monday, February 8, at 9pm ET/6pm PT. The chat home page tells you about upcoming events, and you can also access transcripts of previously held chat sessions.

The upcoming subsections offer detailed instruction for performing tasks relating to Yahoo! as a chat service.

Become a Yahoo! Member

Yahoo! has a very popular chat area. You must become a Yahoo! member to use the chat. To become a Yahoo! member, perform the following steps:

1. From the Yahoo! home page (**www.yahoo.com**), click **Chat**.
2. Click **Sign Me Up**.
3. Read the terms of membership and click the **I Accept** button.
4. Fill out the membership questionnaire in which you create your ID and password. Click **Submit**; your membership is started.

Find and Join a Chat

After you become a Yahoo! member (see the previous section), getting into a chat is very easy. To find and join a chat, perform the following steps:

1. From within your browser, go to the Yahoo! chat page at **chat.yahoo.com**.
2. If asked, enter your membership ID and password (see the previous section).
3. Click a subject area that you want (such as Sports, Romance, Movies).
4. Click the **Start Chatting** button.

Chat at Yahoo!

The Yahoo! chat window is very straightforward. You'll find two windows. The right window contains a list of all the people who are in the chat room. The left window is the chat session, and you'll also find a field for entering your chat. To chat at Yahoo!, perform the following steps:

1. From within a chat room (see the previous section), type your message in the **Chat** field at the bottom of the screen.
2. Click **Send**.
3. Your message appears in the chat window.

USING YAHOO! CHAT

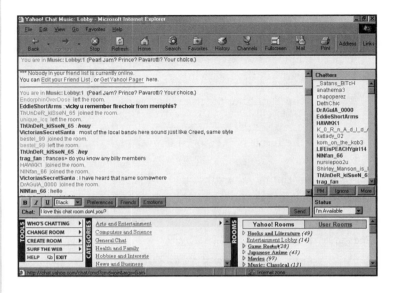

Establish a Private Chat

Sometimes you discover one person in a chat room with whom you would like to have a private conversation. To create a one-on-one chat, perform the following steps:

1. From within a chat session (see "Find and Join a Chat"), click someone's screen name (names are in the right pane).

2. Click the **PM** button (private message) that is located just below the list of chatters.

3. Type in your message.

4. Click **Send**, and the person sees your message on their computer.

Create a Chat Room

You can create your own chat room and invite other users into it. To do so, perform the following steps:

1. From within any chat room (see "Find and Join a Chat"), click the **Create Room** icon.

2. Give your room a name (in the Room Name field).

3. Choose public, private, or secured. (Private rooms do not show in the room list, and chatters cannot enter secure rooms without an invitation.)

4. Click the **Create My Room** button.

INTERNET TELEPHONY AND VIDEOCONFERENCING

One of the hottest growth areas of the Internet is Internet telephony. Basically, the Internet becomes the network for making (and receiving) telephone calls. The big advantage? Price. Using the Internet is a lot cheaper than using standard phone systems. In fact, many companies are working to bring Internet-based telephone services to your regular phone. For the purpose of this book, we'll focus on products and software that you can add to your PC to make phone calls with your PC.

Another big growth area for Internet communications is videoconferencing. As the communication lines that you use to connect to the Internet continue to get faster, it becomes possible to have a high-quality videoconference with your family, friends, or business colleagues. The most current video cameras are in color.

Following are some basic requirements for conducting either a telephone or videoconference via the Internet:

- Microphone
- Camera (only for videoconferencing)
- Speakers and sound card (two sound cards if you want simultaneous two-way conversation as opposed to one person talking at a time)
- Internet phone/videoconferencing software

Don't even try videoconferencing with a modem slower than 56K. Video image quality remains shaky until you get about 112Kbps, which is either an ISDN line, cable modem, or ADSL (see Section I, "Kickstart," for overviews on these access options). At this point, high-speed Internet access comes in handy. In most cases, the person or people whom you are connecting with need to have the same telephone/videoconferencing software on their PC. And, it might sound obvious, but you both need to be online at the same time.

The upcoming subsections offer a few reviews of popular phone and videoconferencing software. Most of these products offer demo software that you can download from their Web site. Microsoft's NetMeeting is free and works with both Internet Explorer and Outlook Express.

NOTE

You can purchase a black-and-white video camera for your PC for as little as $50; color video cameras start at around $100. Try `www.quickcam.com` to learn about the Logitech PC cameras (formerly Connectix).

DigiPhone

DigiPhone Deluxe (`www.digiphone.com`) is an Internet phone software system that provides full-duplex (two-way), real-time audio conversation over the Internet (see Table 14 for a basic list of its features and feature descriptions). You use email addresses to locate and connect with other users. DigiPhone Deluxe comes with a suite of Internet tools including a Telnet program for remote connections and an FTP program to download and transfer files between computers. You get two copies (so you can give one to a friend).

Table 14
DigiPhone Features

Feature	Description
Full-duplex	Simultaneous two-way conversation
Call screening	Accept only the calls you want
Personal phone book	Store names and Internet addresses
Global phone book	Global DigiPhone phone book

Feature	Description
Caller ID	Identifies the caller with text
Message sender	Leave a text message if no answer
Adjustable compression	Optimizes performance
LAN/WAN compatible	Works on TCP/IP networks

SayIt! is another DigiPhone software program that works on your system just as an audio recorder. SayIt! compresses your voice into a sound file (.wav) that you email to other people. Because .wav files are a standard audio file format, the person who receives your audio email doesn't need any special software.

VocalTec

VocalTec (**www.vocaltec.com**) was one of the first companies to offer Internet phone software. The current release lets you see the person you're talking to in video or call someone on a regular telephone (see Table 15 for a basic list of its features and feature descriptions).

Table 15
VocalTec Features

Feature	Description
Full-duplex	Simultaneous two-way conversation
Whiteboard	Enables you to share and edit documents
File transfer	Exchanges files
Text chat	Chat with other users
Global directory	Global user directory
Voice mail	Sends a voice message via email
Video support	See other users with video

CU-SeeMe

Originally developed at Cornell University, CU-SeeMe (**www.wpine.com**) is very popular Internet videoconferencing software (see Table 16 for a basic list of its features and feature descriptions). CU-SeeMe V3.1.2 includes a contact list feature, which means you don't need to know the IP address of the person you want to contact—only their email address. This feature makes it possible to find people using Microsoft NetMeeting 2.1 (see "Using NetMeeting"), and automatically launches NetMeeting 2.1 on your computer (if you have it installed) to contact others using NetMeeting.

Table 16
CU-SeeMe Features

Feature	Description
Directory service	See all users on an ILS server
Caller ID	Screens incoming calls
Directory service	Locates other CU-SeeMe users
Multiple windows	Up to 12 video windows
Phone book	Stores contact information
Whiteboard	Enables you to share and edit documents

UNIFIED MESSAGING

Unified messaging is a concept for those who have to check email, voice mail, faxes, pagers—each with a different technology. Unified messaging enables the Internet, and specifically a Web site, to become your one-stop location for receiving all your messages. Several companies offer Web-based services that enable you to forward your faxes and voice mail to a Web site, or check your email messages via a regular telephone. With unified messaging services, you can always access all the different messages that you receive.

108

UNIFIED MESSAGING

> **NOTE**
>
> Most unified messaging services charge a monthly service fee, although some free services do exist. Make sure you know the terms, conditions, and pricing before you jump in.

Several Internet sites and software programs are available to help provide unified messaging. The following sections provide overviews of these sites and applications.

JFAX

JFAX is both a Web site and a unified messaging service. You pay a small monthly fee for its services. When you subscribe to JFAX (`www.jfax.com`), you get a unique and private phone/fax number in any city in their network. Both your voice mail and faxes are received at this location and then sent to your email. Voice mail plays on your speakers, and the faxes display onscreen. You can save, forward, or delete messages. For unlimited inbound service, the cost is approximately $12.50 a month.

JTALK is another service provided by JFAX. It provides telephone-based access to your email (you only need a touch-tone phone). Call a phone number and you can listen to your email messages being read by a computer. This feature costs approximately $2.50 per month plus 25 cents per minute.

Telebot

Telebot (`www.telebot.net`) is a Web site/service that offers free Internet telephony and unified messaging services to, as their Web site declares, "Everyone, Everywhere." Services include the following:

- Place and receive voice or fax messages through a telephone number in the United States.
- Access voice and fax messages either through a browser or an HTML-compatible email client.
- Receive page notification of incoming email on your pager, PCs, or GSM mobile phone.

A premium service is toll-free voice mail. This service receives your voice messages at a telephone extension on the TeleBot's toll-free (888) phone number (in the U.S.), and then forwards it to your email as a sound file (.wav) attachment.

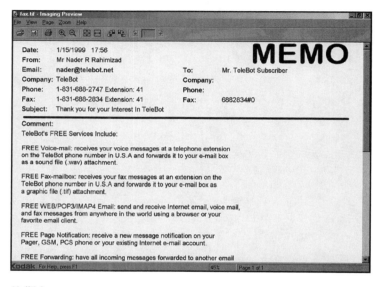

MailTel

If you need to stay in touch with email when you're on the road, or want to be notified when email arrives, MailTel (**www.mailtel.com**) might be your answer. It reads your email to you from any touch-tone phone. When MailTel finds a new message, it copies the message to a MailTel host computer and leaves the original on your email service. You connect to the MailTel network with a phone call and MailTel's text-to-speech conversion software translates the email into a voice that you can hear over the telephone. MailTel also enables you to fax an email message. You also can be paged when new messages arrive.

USING MICROSOFT NETMEETING

NetMeeting (a Microsoft software product) provides both Internet telephone and videoconferencing capabilities via the Internet. For the phone feature, you need a sound card, speakers, and a microphone. For video, add a Video for Windows-compatible video capture card and/or a video camera.

NetMeeting also provides data conferencing. You can collaborate with a group of people from within any Windows application. You can transfer control of the application from one location to another (for example, to let someone in a remote location work on your Excel spreadsheet). You can draw and share images on a shared whiteboard, send text messages, and transfer files. Table 17 offers a basic list of NetMeeting features and feature descriptions.

Table 17
NetMeeting Features

Feature	Description
Application sharing	Enables multiple users to control application
Chat	Real-time text-based chatting
Whiteboard	Share drawings onscreen
File transfer	Transfer files between locations
Videoconferencing	Full-motion video
Speed-dial directory	Quick access to people you call
ILS directory	Directory of other NetMeeting users

The upcoming subsections offer detailed instructions for performing tasks relating to Microsoft's NetMeeting.

USING MICROSOFT NETMEETING

Quick Tips

Feature	Icon	Keyboard Shortcut
New call		Ctrl+N
Chat		Ctrl+T
Whiteboard		Ctrl+W
ILS directory		Ctrl+D
File transfer		Ctrl+F

Acquire and Launch NetMeeting

The great thing about NetMeeting is the price—free! Just download the latest version from Microsoft's Web site and install. To do so, perform the following steps:

1. Go to **www.microsoft.com/netmeeting**.

2. Click **download latest version**.

3. From the drop-down menu, select the version for your operating system; then click **Next**.

4. Choose a download site, and click **Next**.

5. A File Download screen appears. Choose **Save This Program to Disk** and click **OK**.

6. Choose a location to download this file to your hard drive (if you choose the Desktop, it will be easy to find). Click **Save**. The file is downloaded to your hard drive.

7. After the download is complete, click the icon for NetMeeting installation (find it on your desktop or in the directory you saved it to). This runs the NetMeeting installation wizard where you install the program. During installation, a NetMeeting icon is added to your Programs Directory (usually along with Internet Explorer).

8. Find the NetMeeting icon on the Programs menu (usually under the Internet Explorer group of programs). Double-click to launch.

You can always change any options you might have set up during
installation by choosing **Tools**, then **Options** after you launch
NetMeeting.

Connect and Call with NetMeeting

NetMeeting audio conferencing provides half-duplex (one
person at a time) and full-duplex (simultaneous conversation) audio support for real-time conversations. You will
have better audio quality if your PC has a Pentium processor.
Because NetMeeting supports the H.323 protocol (an international standard for telephone and video devices on
networks), it is interoperable with other H.323-compatible
audio software.

You connect with a server where other people are also connected. A directory server identifies the people whom you
can contact with NetMeeting. NetMeeting provides access
to several directory servers (such as
`http://ils3.microsoft.com`—ils stands for Internet Locator
Service). When you log onto a directory server, other users
see your name and can contact you. For private sessions,
you can prevent people from contacting you when you are
in a NetMeeting session. Your ISP might also offer private
directory servers.

To connect/call with NetMeeting, perform the following
steps:

1. Launch NetMeeting (see the previous section).

2. Click the directory icon at the left side of the screen.

3. Open the server drop-down window and click one of
   the ils servers. Usually the default ils server is busy and
   you might have to try one or two to connect.

4. A directory of current users appears; double-click
   someone's name to call them.

USING MICROSOFT NETMEETING

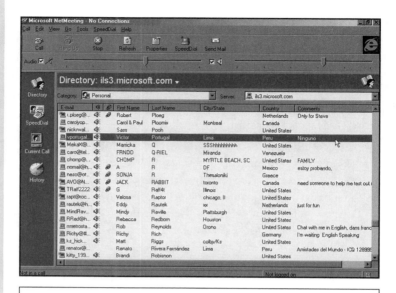

USING MICROSOFT NETMEETING

TIP

Frequently, the other people at an ILS server are either in a conversation with someone else, or they aren't answering calls. The best NetMeeting results are when you have a friend who also connects and you call one another.

Use the Whiteboard

The whiteboard function enables you to share drawings and images with the people you are talking to. You can use your mouse to draw pictures. Using the whiteboard, perform the following steps:

1. From within NetMeeting, choose **Tools**, then **Whiteboard**.

2. Use your mouse to draw images on the whiteboard and select drawing tools and text from the left toolbar. Everyone in the current meeting is able to view and use the whiteboard.

TIP

You can transmit pictures (GIF, JPEG, TIFF, and so on) via the whiteboard by first copying the image (Ctrl+C), and then pasting (Ctrl+V) onto the whiteboard.

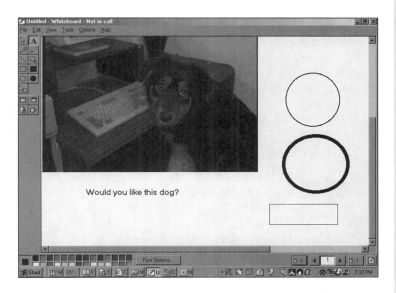

Share an Application

When someone accepts your call, you are both placed in a meeting where you can talk and share data. NetMeeting opens a new toolbar when you are in a call.

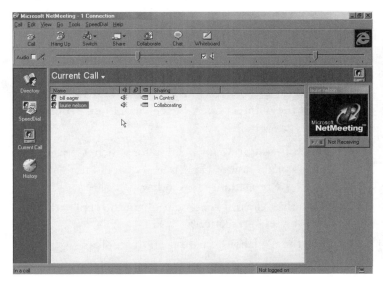

Sharing an application means that the other party can see what you are doing, but cannot take control of the application. For example, you could open a Word document and let them see it on their screen. To share an application, perform the following steps:

1. Launch any software application you want to share. You launch it as you normally would from Windows.

2. Click the **Share** button on the NetMeeting toolbar.

3. Click **OK** on the warning screen that tells you the security issues related to sharing data.

Enable Collaboration

Collaboration allows the other party to actually use your application from their remote location. Before you can collaborate with an application, you must first select it to be shared. Collaboration makes the actual features of the application available to others. The other party controls the software program. This can be a security issue. For example, if they control Microsoft Word, they can open any Word file on your hard drive. You can watch everything other people do as they use your application. Microsoft recommends that you don't leave your PC unattended while in a collaboration because you can't monitor who is doing what to your computer. To stop the person who has control of the shared application from making any changes, press (Esc) or press the mouse button to regain control of the pointer. To enable collaboration, perform the following steps:

1. Launch the software application for which you want to enable collaboration. Do this as you would normally launch the program from Windows.

2. Within NetMeeting, choose to share the application (see the previous section).

3. Click the **Collaborate** button on the toolbar.

4. Click **OK** after the warning screen that discusses the security issues related to collaboration.

5. Click **Collaborate** again to stop the collaboration process.

NOTE

To have a two-way collaboration process, all parties have to click **Share and Collaborate** to begin the sharing and collaboration process. Because you are going through the Internet when you collaborate, the application might seem to work slowly.

Perform File Transfer

You can transfer a file from your hard drive to the hard drive of someone else (with whom you are in a current NetMeeting call). To do so, perform the following steps:

1. From within NetMeeting, choose **Tools**, then **File Transfer**, then **Send File** (or Ctrl+F).

2. Find the file on your hard drive.

3. Click **Send**. The file is transmitted to the other user's PC.

WORLD WIDE WEB

If email and newsgroups are appetizers of the Internet, then the World Wide Web is definitely the main course. The World Wide Web has become the most popular application of the Internet. Why? Because, with a click of your mouse, you can jump from a Web site about horse racing in Kentucky to a site with pictures of the Great Wall of China. The Web is easy to use. You will discover an unlimited variety of information about every subject you can imagine. It also offers multimedia—images, sounds, animation, and video.

The World Wide Web began in 1989 after Swiss physicist Tim Berners-Lee proposed the concept of the Web as a system to transfer ideas and research among scientists around the world. The Web connects computers around the world (just like a spider web). Information that is on any one computer (a Web page) can be connected to any other Web page with an onscreen link. These links can be text or graphics and are known as *hyperlinks*. So, as a user, you use your mouse to visit specific Web sites by entering their address into a software program called a Web browser. The two most popular Web browsers are Netscape Communicator and Microsoft Internet Explorer. You can also jump from one Web site to another with the hyper-links. The big advantage of the Web as an Internet system is the ease-of-use of hyperlinks and the fact that multimedia is available.

In addition to just straightforward information, Web sites now offer applications for accomplishing tasks. These include creating your own Web site, searching for friends, getting the best deal on an airline ticket, investing in stock, and purchasing products. Electronic commerce is growing rapidly. Zona Research predicts that the revenue from Internet transactions will grow from approximately $25 bil-lion in 1998 to more than $200 billion in the year 2001. Section VII, "Web Resources: Find It on the Internet," goes into great detail on these more advanced Web services. This section is dedicated to the more general navigation of and features of the Web. Specifically, this section addresses the following main topic areas:

- Definitions
- Speed Issues
- Using America Online
- Using Internet Explorer
- Using Netscape Navigator
- Software That Works with Your Browser

DEFINITIONS

Following are definitions of common Web terms:

- **Browser**   The software program you use to view Web sites.
- **Cookie**   A small file that is saved on your hard drive that contains information a Web site might need for login, credit card, address, or user preferences.
- **Home page**   The starting page for a Web site.
- **HTML**   Short for Hypertext Markup Language—the coding language of the Web.
- **Link**   A word or image on a Web page that you can click to jump to another page or Web resource (such as a file).
- **Page**   One individual page within a Web site.
- **Plug-In**   A software program that works in conjunction with a browser to perform a specific application.
- **Portal**   A Web site that offers a variety of services (such as searching, email, and news) and becomes a gateway to the Internet for users.
- **Search engine**   A Web site that helps you search the Web for sites that meet your criteria or keywords.
- **Sourcecode**   The HTML code that creates a Web page.
- **Streaming**   When audio or video is fed continuously to your PC from a Web site (it streams in).
- **Surf**   Casually jumping from one Web site to another without any specific intentions.

122

- **URL** Uniform Resource Locator (a Web address).
- **Webmaster** A person who creates or programs Web pages for a site.

SPEED ISSUES

If you don't have high-speed Internet access, the Web can sometimes be a frustrating experience because of the time it takes for Web pages to load. Following are a few tips that might help you in the speed arena:

- **Peak hours** Try to avoid Internet peak hours. Just as with a highway, when lots of people are online simultaneously, the Internet slows down. Noontime and weekends tend to be peak hours.

- **Turn off graphics** If you really want to move fast, you can turn off your browser's display of graphics so that you see only text as you move from site to site.

- **Site overload** Individual sites can also slow down. Either because too many people are using them, or the connection to the computer for the site has slowed down. Try later.

- **Cache** Cache refers to the amount of space that you reserve on your hard disk to store information and images of Web sites you visit. The advantage of cache is that when you visit a page that has been cached, it loads much faster the second time. The disadvantages are that the site might have new information (click Refresh or Reload to update the page) or you are using up space on your hard drive. Most browsers enable you to determine the amount of cache you want. If your computer doesn't have a lot of extra hard drive space, then Internet files that are cached can actually slow down your PC. There is no right amount of disk space to reserve for the cache (also known as Temporary Internet Files). It really depends on how large your hard drive is and what percentage you are comfortable reserving for this purpose. You can always delete the entire cache to clear up this space.

- **PC and modem performance** The capability of your PC to rapidly process information from a Web site can have an impact on the speed at which you surf. Likewise, a faster modem means faster downloads. Upgrade your modem to 56Kbps. Add more RAM to your PC. Upgrade to a Pentium.

USING AMERICA ONLINE

The popular online service America Online (AOL) provides easy access to the Web, with a browser that has enough features and options to get you where you want to go.

The upcoming subsections offer detailed instructions for performing tasks relating to AOL's World Wide Web browser.

Open a Web Site

There are three ways to launch the AOL browser and open a Web site. Perform the following steps:

1. Launch and sign onto America Online.
2. Click the **Internet** button on the toolbar.
3. Choose **Go to the Web**.
4. The AOL home page opens.

or

1. Launch and sign onto America Online.
2. Click in the Keyword field (just below the toolbar).
3. Type a Web address (you don't need **http://**).
4. Press ⏎Enter on your keyboard.
5. The site you chose opens.

124

or

1. Launch and sign onto America Online.
2. Click the (Home) button on the Web toolbar.
3. Your default home page opens.

NOTE

If you select Internet, then AOL Netfind, you reach an AOL Web site that offers both a search engine as well as several online directories for email and newsgroup searching.

Set AOL to Launch a New Start Page

Your start page (the page that opens when you click (Home) on the Web toolbar) can be changed to any site you like. To change it, perform the following steps:

1. From within AOL, choose the **My AOL** button on the toolbar, then **Preferences**.
2. Click the **WWW** icon.
3. Click the **General** tab.

USING AMERICA ONLINE

4. In the Home Page Address field, either type the URL of the site you want, or click **Use Current** to make the current page the start page.

Create Favorites

AOL helps you save a list of the sites that you like, so you can return to them quickly. These are called *Favorites*. To add a site to your Favorites list, perform the following steps:

1. Open a Web site that you want as a Favorite.
2. Click the **Favorites** button on the toolbar.
3. Select **Add Top Window to Favorite Places**.
4. Click **Add to Favorites**.

or

1. Open a Web site that you want as a Favorite.
2. Click the heart icon at the top of the browser window.
3. Click **Add to Favorites**.

Open Favorites

After you have added a site to your Favorites list (see the previous section), you can open it easily at any time. To access a site by way of your Favorites list, perform the following steps:

1. From within AOL, click the **Favorites** button on the toolbar.
2. Select **Favorite Places**.
3. Double-click the name of the site you want to open.

Organize Favorites

The more you use your AOL browser, chances are the more favorites you will have (see section "Create Favorites"). To make it easier to navigate your Favorites list, you can set it up so that those favorites are organized into folders. To organize your Favorites this way, perform the following steps:

1. From within AOL, click the **Favorites** button on the toolbar.

126

2. Select **Favorite Places**.

3. Click **New** to create a new favorite or a new Folder for favorites. If you are creating a new favorite, enter the URL and the name; for a folder, enter only the name. Then click **OK** to create it.

4. To move existing favorites from one folder to another, simply click the favorite and drag it to the folder you want. Or, click it and press the Del button on your keyboard to get rid of the favorite.

TIP

From the Favorite Places window, you can highlight and drag a favorite site from one folder to another.

Create Multiple Browser Windows

It's easy to get several browser windows going at one time. To open a new window, perform the following steps:

1. From within your AOL browser, right-click a link on a Web page.

2. Choose **Open in New Window**.

Email a Web Page

When you find the perfect Web page, you might want to share it with a friend. To email a Web page, perform the following steps:

1. Open the Web page you want to share.

2. Click the heart icon at the top of the browser window.

3. Click **Insert in Mail**.

4. Type your friend's email address.

5. Click **Send Now**.

Save a Web Page

There might be an occasion when you want to save a Web page to your hard drive for future reference. The advantage to this is that you can always open the page (even when you are not online). And, if the site should delete the page, you'll still have your copy. To save a Web page to disk, perform the following steps:

1. Open the Web page you want to save.

2. Choose **File**, then **Save**.

3. Type a filename, select the directory within which to save the page, and click **Save**.

Set Disk Space for Temporary Internet Files

Every time you visit a Web page, AOL saves the HTML and the images in a Temporary Internet Folder on your hard drive. This makes these pages load much faster the next time you visit them. Unfortunately it can also consume a large portion of your hard drive. So you need to tell AOL how much of your hard drive you want to reserve for this purpose. To set this space, perform the following steps:

1. From within AOL, click the **My AOL** button on the toolbar, then **Preferences**.

2. Click the icon labeled **WWW**.

3. On the General tab under Temporary Internet Files, click **Settings**.

4. Slide the ruler to select the **Amount of Disk Space to Use**. A good starting point is 10% of the drive.

5. Click **OK**.

Delete Temporary Internet Files

One way to control the amount of space taken up by temporary Internet files is to set a determined amount of space allotted for them (see previous section). Another way is to simply delete them from time to time. To delete temporary Internet files, perform the following steps:

1. From within AOL, click the **My AOL** button on the toolbar, then **Preferences**.
2. Click the icon labeled **WWW**.
3. Under Temporary Internet Files (on the General Tab), click **Delete Files**.

USING INTERNET EXPLORER

Microsoft's Web browser, Internet Explorer, makes it easy to navigate the World Wide Web. Features include the capability to add a list of favorite sites for easy access, printing, and emailing Web sites.

The upcoming subsections offer detailed instructions for performing tasks related to the use of Internet Explorer as a World Wide Web browser.

Quick Tips

Feature	Button	Keyboard Shortcut
Open page		Ctrl+O
Back one page	Back	Alt+←
Refresh the page	Refresh	F5
New browser window		Ctrl+N
Open new window from link		Shift+Click on Link
Organize Favorites		Ctrl+B
Show full page		F11
Print page	Print	Ctrl+P

Open a Web Site

There are a couple of different ways to open a Web site
with Internet Explorer. The browser helps you quickly
access a new site, jump to a home page that you can establish (see next section), open a site that you save in a list of
favorite sites (see "Create Favorites"), or find a site that
you visited in the past three weeks. To open a new site,
perform the following steps:

1. Click in the Address field just below the toolbar.
2. Enter the URL or Web address for the site (you don't
   need to type the **http://**, only the address).
3. Press ⏎Enter on your keyboard, and the site opens.

To jump to your home page (see the next section), perform
the following:

1. Click the Home button on the toolbar. The default Start
   Page opens.

To open a Favorite site (see "Create Favorites"), perform
the following steps:

1. Click the **Favorites** button on the toolbar.
2. The Favorites list opens. Scroll down to a Favorites link
   saved on the Favorites menu.
3. Click the favorite site you want to see. The site opens.

To view a site you've seen in the past three weeks, perform
the following steps:

1. Click the **History** button on the toolbar.
2. The History list opens (this is a list of sites that you
   have visited over the past three weeks). Scroll down
   and select a week or day, and then a specific Web site
   that you visited.
3. Click the link, and the site opens.

Set Internet Explorer to Launch a New Start Page

The first time you use Internet Explorer, it creates its own default start page at Microsoft. This is the first Web site you see when you launch Internet Explorer. You might want to have another Web site be your start page. To set Internet Explorer to launch a new start page, perform the following steps:

1. From within the browser, open the Web page you want to become the new start page.
2. Choose **View**, then **Internet Options**.
3. In the Home Page area, click the **Use Current** button.
4. Click **OK** to accept.

Create Favorites

Internet Explorer helps you save a list of the sites that you like so that you can return to them quickly. These sites are called Favorites. To add a site to your Favorites list, perform the following steps:

1. Open a Web site that you think you'll want to visit again.

2. Choose **Favorites**, then **Add to Favorites**.

3. Click **OK** to add to the list of favorites.

TIP

You can add a Favorite with one keystroke. Just press Ctrl+D. The page is automatically added to your Favorites list without any further input from you.

Create Favorites in Folders

In addition to adding a site to your general Favorites list (see the previous section), you can add a site to a specific folder within the Favorites list. To do so, perform the following steps:

1. Open a Web site that you think you'll want to visit again.

2. Choose **Favorites,** then **Add to Favorites**.

3. Click **Create In**; a list of existing folders appears.

4. Either click one of these folders or click **New Folder** to create a new one.

5. If you clicked one of the existing folders, all you need to do is click **OK** to place the Web page in that folder. If you create a new folder, enter the name of the folder in the **Folder Name** field.

6. Click **OK** to create the folder, then **OK** again to place the Web page in the new folder.

Create Favorites for Files on Your Hard Drive

You can also create Favorites (see "Create Favorites") that are shortcuts to open files that exist on your hard drive. To do so, perform the following steps:

1. From within the browser, choose **File** then **Open**.

2. Click **Browse**; then navigate through your C: drive directory to locate the file you want.

3. Double-click the filename; then click **OK** to open the file in Internet Explorer.

4. Choose **Favorites**, then **Add to Favorites**, then **OK**. The file is now added to your list of favorites and you can open it with Internet Explorer.

Set Up Automatic Notification of Updates to Favorites

Internet Explorer can send you an email notice when one of your Favorite pages (see "Create Favorites") gets updated with new information. To activate this automatic notification, perform the following steps:

1. Open the Web site you want to be notified about.
2. Choose **Favorites**, then **Add to Favorites**.
3. Click **Yes, but Only Tell Me When This Page Is Updated**. If you select this option, the favorite shows that the page has new information.
4. Or, if you want the page automatically downloaded, click **Yes, Notify Me of Updates and Download the Page for Offline Viewing**.
5. Click **Customize**.
6. When asked whether you want to be notified in an email message, check **Yes**.
7. Click **Next**.
8. Enter your email address and email server (such as mail.rmi.net).
9. Click **Next**.
10. If the site requires a username and password, enter yours.
11. Click **Finish,** then **OK**. You now get email notification when the site offers updated information.

Organize, Rename, Delete Favorites

Internet Explorer makes it easy for you to organize (and reorganize) your favorite sites (see "Create Favorites"). To organize your Favorites, perform the following steps:

1. From within the browser, choose **Favorites**, then **Organize Favorites**.
2. Click a Favorites folder or shortcut.

3. Drag an item you want to reposition to a new folder of your choice.

4. Use **Move**, **Rename**, or **Delete** buttons to further modify your Favorites.

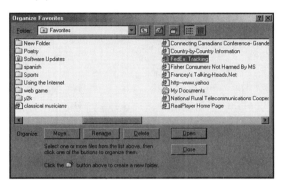

Customize the Links Bar

The links bar is the bottom bar on the Toolbar, under the Address field. This bar allows you to have a few icons for sites you really want to visit quickly. You just click them, and they open. Internet Explorer comes with several preset links, such as Channel Guide and Internet Start. You can add your own favorite sites to this bar. To do so, perform the following steps:

1. Open the site or Web page that you want to add to the links bar.

2. Drag the icon for the page (which is just to the left of the address in the address field) onto the Links bar. The Web site is added to the Links bar with a little icon, and you can now just click this to open the site.

TIP

To remove a link from the Links bar, right-click it and click Del.

Open a New Browser Window

Sometimes you'll want to have more than one Internet Explorer browser window open—either to view two sites simultaneously or to keep one site available while you go somewhere else. To open a new window, perform the following steps:

1. From a site within the browser, press ⒸⓉⓇⓁ+Ⓝ to launch a new window.
2. Enter the new Web site address in the Address field.
3. Press ⏎Enter on your keyboard and the site opens.

Open New Browser Window from Link

You can open a new browser window (see the previous section) from a link. To do so, perform the following step:

1. At a site within the browser, press and hold down the ⇧Shift key as you click a link at that site. The new site or page opens in a new window.

TIP

To view several Internet Explorer Windows simultaneously, right-click an empty part of the taskbar, which is the bar at the bottom of the screen, and click either Tile Windows Horizontally or Tile Windows Vertically.

Email a Web Page or Link

You might, on occasion, find a Web page or video or audio clip that you want to send to someone via email. To do so, perform the following steps:

1. Open the page you want to send.
2. Choose **File**, then **Send**, then either **Page by Email** to send a copy of the page or **Link by Email** to send a shortcut to the page.
3. Your default email program opens. Enter the email address for the person you want to send the page or link to.
4. Add a message if you want.
5. Click **Send**.

Save a Web Page As HTML

Sometimes you'll want to save a Web page for future reference. The following procedure saves the HTML of a Web page (the code for the page) on your disk drive. The advantage to this is that you can always open the page (even when you are not online). And, if the site should delete the page, you'll still have your copy. The images, however, are not saved, just the text and the formatting. To save a page as HTML, perform the following steps:

1. Open the page you want to save.
2. Choose **File**, then **Save As**.
3. Type a filename, select the directory within which you want to save this page to, and click **Save**.

Save a Web Page in Microsoft Word

Internet Explorer provides a convenient way to open a Web page (text and links) in Microsoft Word. You might want to do this if you want to have some of the text in a word processor format, or if you want to edit the page and save it in HTML format on your hard drive. To save a Web page in Microsoft Word, perform the following steps:

1. Open the page you want to export to Microsoft Word.
2. Click the **Edit** button on the Toolbar.
3. Within Microsoft Word, you can now save the page as Word file (or HTML) with standard Microsoft Word Save.

View HTML Source Code (and Save As Text File)

If you are interested in how a Web page is created (HTML code), then view the source code for the page. It's easy. Perform the following steps:

1. Open the Web page for which you want to see source code.
2. Choose **View**, then **Source**. Source code opens in Notepad.
3. Choose **File**, then **Save** to save as text file.

Download a File

Many times you will come across a file that you want to download. The file could be a software program, a word processing file, a music file, a video file—anything, really. You access a file the same way you do a Web page, by clicking a link to download the file to your hard drive. After you have downloaded the file, you can view it, listen to it, or install it (software). To download a file, perform the following steps:

1. Locate a file on a Web site you want to download.

2. Click the link to start the download.

3. A Save As window opens. Choose the directory within which you want to save the file, and click **Save**.

4. The file begins to download to your PC; a download status bar appears. When download is complete, the status bar disappears.

5. Go to the directory where you saved the file to open it (usually by double-clicking it).

Set Disk Space for Temporary Internet Files

Every time you visit a Web page, Internet Explorer saves the HTML and the images in a Temporary Internet Folder on your hard drive. This makes these pages load much faster the next time you visit them. Unfortunately, it can also consume a large portion of your hard drive. So, you need to tell Internet Explorer how much of your hard drive you want to reserve for this purpose. To set this space, perform the following steps:

1. From within Internet Explorer, choose **View**, then **Internet Options**.

2. Under **Temporary Internet Files** (on the General Tab) click **Settings**.

3. Slide the ruler to select the **Amount of Disk Space to Use**. Most users select about 10% of the disk drive for storage.

4. Click **OK**.

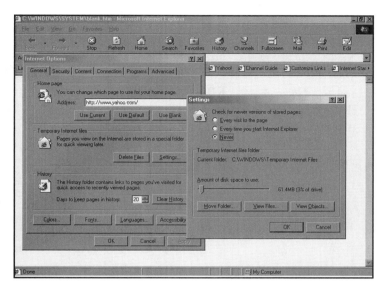

Delete Temporary Internet Files

One way to control the amount of space taken up by temporary Internet files is to set a determined amount of space allotted for them (see the previous section). Another way is to simply delete them from time to time. To delete temporary Internet files, perform the following steps:

1. From within Internet Explorer, choose **View**, then **Internet Options**.

2. Under Temporary Internet Files (on the General Tab), click **Delete Files**.

NOTE

You can also get to the Temporary Internet Files folder with Windows Explorer. The default is C:/Windows/Temporary Internet Files.

USING NETSCAPE NAVIGATOR

The browser Netscape Navigator offers features that include saving sites you use frequently for easy access, emailing Web pages, viewing the HTML source code for Web pages, and more.

138

The upcoming subsections offer detailed instructions for
performing tasks relating to the use of Netscape Navigator
as a World Wide Web browser.

Quick Tips	
Feature	*Keyboard Shortcut*
Open page	Ctrl+O
Save page	Ctrl+S
Add a bookmark	Ctrl+D
Edit bookmarks	Ctrl+B
Select all on a page	Ctrl+A
Find in a page	Ctrl+F
View source code	Ctrl+U
Reload page	Ctrl+R
Information about a page	Ctrl+I
Print a page	Ctrl+P

Open a Web Site

There are a couple of different ways to open a Web site
with Netscape Navigator. The browser helps you quickly
access a new site, jump to a home page that you can establish (see the next section), or open a site that you save in a
list of favorite sites (see "Create Bookmarks"). To open a
new site, perform the following steps:

1. Click in the Location field just below the toolbar.
2. Enter the URL or Web address for the site (you don't
   need to type the **http://**, only the address).
3. Press ⏎Enter on your keyboard, and the site opens.

To jump to your home page (see the next section), perform
the following steps:

1. Click the Home button on the toolbar. The default Start
   Page opens.

USING NAVIGATOR

To open a favorite site (see "Create Bookmarks"), perform the following steps:

1. Click **Bookmarks** next to the Location field.

2. The Bookmarks list opens. Scroll down to a Bookmarks link saved on the menu.

3. Click the bookmarks site you want to see. The site opens.

Set Netscape Navigator to Launch a New Start Page

The first time you use Netscape Navigator, it creates its own default start page at Microsoft. This is the first Web site you see when you launch Netscape Navigator. You might want to have another Web site be your start page. To set Netscape Navigator to launch a new start page, perform the following steps:

1. From within the browser, open the Web page you want to become the new start page.

2. Choose **Edit**, then **Preferences**.

3. In the Home Page area, click the **Use Current Page** button.

4. Click **OK** to accept.

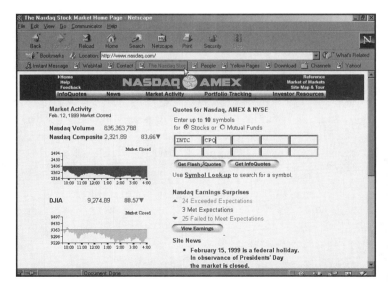

Launch the Floating Component Bar

Although it's an awkward name—Floating Component Bar—it is a good feature. Netscape lets you launch a little navigation tool that sits on top of all applications (including Netscape). The bar includes buttons to help you quickly jump to (or launch) Navigator, Email Inbox, Newsgroups, your Address Book, and Composer (a Web page creation tool.) To launch this feature, perform the following steps:

1. From within Netscape, choose **View**, then **Show**.
2. Click **Floating Component Bar**.

Create Bookmarks

Netscape Navigator helps you save a list of the sites that you like, so you can return to them quickly. These are called Bookmarks. To add a site to your Bookmarks list, perform the following steps:

1. Open a Web site that you think you'll want to visit again.
2. Choose **Communicator**, then **Bookmarks**, then **Add Bookmark**.

TIP

You can add a Favorite with one keystroke. Just press Ctrl+D. The page is automatically added to your Favorites list without any further input from you.

Create Bookmarks in Categories

In addition to adding a site to your general Bookmarks list (see the previous section), you can add a site to a specific category within the Bookmarks list. To do so, perform the following steps:

1. Open a Web site that you think you'll want to visit again.

2. Choose **Communicator**, then **Bookmarks**, then **File Bookmark**.

3. Click the folder (or category) you want to save the bookmark in.

Create a New Bookmark Category

You can create new Folders for your bookmarks (see "Create Bookmarks"). For example, you might want a Folder called Nature Sites where you can bookmark all the sites for state parks. To create a custom folder, perform the following steps:

1. From within Netscape Navigator, choose **Communicator**, then **Bookmarks**, then **Edit Bookmarks**.

2. Choose **File**, then **New Folder**.

3. Type the Folder name, then click **OK**.

Organize Bookmarks

Netscape Navigator makes it easy for you to organize your bookmarked sites (see "Create Bookmarks"). To do so, perform the following steps:

1. From within Netscape Navigator, choose **Communicator**, then **Bookmarks**, then **Edit Bookmarks**.

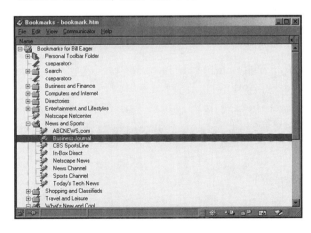

2. Highlight any bookmark and drag it from one folder to another. You can also delete bookmarks by simply clicking them and then hitting the Del key on your keyboard.

Customize the Links Bar

The Links bar is the bottom bar on the Toolbar, under the Address field. This bar allows you to have a few icons for sites you really want to visit quickly. You just click them and they open. Netscape Navigator comes with several preset links such as People and Yellow Pages. You can add your own favorite sites to this bar. To do so, perform the following steps:

1. Open the site or Web page that you want to add to the Links bar.

2. Drag the bookmarks icon for the page (which is just to the left of the address in the address field) onto the Links bar. (Your cursor turns into a little hand when you move it over the bookmarks icon.) Now you can quickly access the site(s) by clicking them on the Links bar.

Open a New Browser Window

Sometimes you'll want to have more than one Netscape Navigator browser window open—either to view two sites simultaneously or to keep one site available while you go somewhere else. To open a new window, perform the following steps:

1. From a site within the browser, press Ctrl+N to launch a new window.

2. Enter the new Web site address in the Address field.

3. Press ↵Enter on your keyboard, and the site opens.

Email a Web Page or Link

It's easy to send (email) someone a link to a Web page you like. Perform the following steps:

1. Open the page you want to send.
2. Choose **File**, then **Send Page**.
3. Fill in the address field on the Mail Composition screen.
4. Click **Send**.

Save a Web Page As HTML

Sometimes you'll want to save a Web page for future reference. The advantage to this is that you can always open the page (even when you are not online). And, if the site should delete the page, you'll still have your copy. The following procedure saves the HTML (source code for the page) of a Web page on your disk drive. It doesn't, however, save the images that are part of the page, only the text and the formatting. To save a page as HTML, perform the following steps:

1. Open the page you want to save.
2. Choose **File**, then **Save As**.
3. Type a filename, the directory within which you want to save the page, and Click **Save**.

View HTML Source Code

To learn how a Web page is created (the HTML code), you'll need to view the source code for the page. To do so, perform the following steps:

1. Open the Web page you want to see source code for.
2. Choose **View**, then **Page Source**.
3. Source code opens in a Netscape window. If you want, use Windows copy ((Ctrl)+(C)) and paste ((Ctrl)+(V)) to save the source code to another file.

144

```
Source of: http://www.nasdaq.com/ - Netscape                          _ 8 X
<HTML>
<HEAD>
         <META HTTP-EQUIV="Content-Type" content="text/html; charset=iso-8859-1">
    <META NAME="Classification" CONTENT="Nasdaq Stock Market Information">
    <META NAME="Rating" CONTENT="General">
    <META NAME="Revisit-after" CONTENT="daily">
    <META NAME="Updated" CONTENT="daily">
    <META NAME="Distribution" CONTENT="Global">
    <META NAME="ObjectType" CONTENT="Document">
    <META NAME="Robots" CONTENT="ALL">
    <META NAME="Publisher" CONTENT="NASDAQ">
    <META NAME="AUTHOR" CONTENT="Text/notepad (TKMSA;JBH1) [Netscape, MSIE,AOL, Mosaic]">
    <META NAME="Search Engines" CONTENT="AltaVista, AOLNet, Infoseek, Excite, Hotbot, Lycos,
    <META NAME="GENERATOR" CONTENT="Mozilla/3.01Gold (WinNT; U) [Netscape]">

    <META NAME="DESCRIPTION" CONTENT="Nasdaq Stock Market">
    <TITLE>The Nasdaq Stock Market Home Page</TITLE>
</HEAD>

<!--- start of file popstart.inc --->
<!--- file:popadjscommon.inc  Common -->
<HEAD>
<SCRIPT LANGUAGE="JavaScript">


<!--- Hide
function myOnErr(msg, url,lno) {if (gbCh) {gbCh=0; return true;} return false;}
function noError(msg,url,lno) {return true;}
var gsBr='old';var gbOj=1;
var gbCk=0;var gsToUrl= '';
var POP_CKY='popad';var AD_DATE='date';
var ST_SHOW=1;var ST_LATEP=2;var ST_DONE=3;var ST_DONT=4;
var AD_EXP=60;var CKY_EXP=90;
var PARENT_EXT='NasdaqMain';
```

Download a File

Many times you come across a file that you want to download. The file could be a software program, a word processing file, a music file, a video file—anything, really. You access a file the same way you do a Web page, by clicking a link to download the file to your hard drive. After you have downloaded the file, you can view it, listen to it, or install it (software). To download a file, perform the following steps:

1. Locate a file on a Web site you want to download.
2. Click the link to start the download.
3. A Save As window opens. Choose the directory within which you want to save the file, and click **Save**.
4. The file begins to download to your PC; a download status bar appears. When download is complete, the status bar disappears.
5. Go to the directory where you saved the file to open it (usually by double-clicking it).

USING NAVIGATOR

Set Disk Space for Internet Cache

Every time you visit a Web page, Netscape Navigator saves the HTML and the images on your hard drive. This makes these pages load much faster the next time you visit them. Unfortunately, it can also consume a large portion of your hard drive. So, you need to tell Netscape Navigator how much of your hard drive you want to reserve for this purpose (cache). To set this cache space, perform the following steps:

1. From within Netscape Navigator, choose **Edit**, then **Preferences**.
2. In the Category window, click **Advanced**.
3. Click **Cache**.
4. The disk cache is the cache for your hard drive. Type your preference and click OK. (Netscape default is approximately 8MB, which is a good starting point.)

NOTE

You can also increase or decrease your memory cache—this is the cache that is stored in RAM.

Delete Cache Files

One way to control the amount of space taken up by cache files is to set a determined amount of space allotted (see the previous section). Another way is to simply delete them from time to time. To delete cache files, perform the following steps:

1. From within Netscape, choose **Edit**, then **Preferences**.
2. In the Category window, click **Advanced**.
3. Click **Cache**.
4. Click either (or both) **Clear Memory Cache** or **Clear Disk Cache**.

SOFTWARE THAT WORKS WITH YOUR BROWSER

There are several software programs that work in conjunction with your Web browser to enrich your online experience. They enrich it because they enable multimedia, or audio/video, or a better version of onscreen print materials. Some of these programs launch when you click a hyperlink to the type of media that they can play; others work in the background, and you might not even know that they are working. The following sections provide an overview of the most popular and powerful programs that work with your browser and provide instructions on downloading the latest versions of some of these programs.

RealPlayer

Real Networks is a company that has helped advance the use of audio and video on the Internet. They make a very popular software program called RealPlayer. RealPlayer lets you listen to audio and view video that uses a process called *streaming.* Streaming media plays very quickly even over slower connections (28.8Kpbs) because the media is sent continuously in little bits—a stream—to your PC. RealPlayer works with America Online, Internet Explorer, and Netscape Navigator Web browsers. What this means is that if you use AOL, Internet Explorer, or Netscape Navigator to visit a Web site that has streaming media (audio and video), the RealPlayer program automatically launches and plays the media for you.

You will find both a free version of RealPlayer and a version that you can pay for called RealPlayer Plus (about $30). RealPlayer Plus offers a few advantages including a hi-fi audio display with a 10-channel equalizer to tune treble, bass, and midrange. RealPlayer Plus also enables you to control the picture quality of RealVideo with video controls for brightness, contrast, saturation, hue, and sharpness.

To get the latest version of RealPlayer, perform the following steps:

1. Go to the Real Networks Web site at `www.real.com`.
2. Click the home page link to **Products**.
3. Under the area for Players, click the **Download** link.
4. Click the link for **RealPlayer** (or **RealPlayer Plus**).
5. Fill out the registration form that asks for your name, email address, country, operating system, CPU, language, and access speed.
6. Click **Download RealPlayer**. RealPlayer downloads to the directory you choose.
7. After you download it, you need to go to the file and double-click it to run the RealPlayer installation wizard to install the software on your PC.

Shockwave

Shockwave has become the standard for multimedia play-back on the Web. It is a software program that helps you view interactive content—including games, business presentations, and entertainment—with a Web browser. Indeed, because Shockwave creates fun animations and interactive presentations, many Web sites use Shockwave.

After you have Shockwave installed on your PC, it automatically works with your Web browser to enable you to view Shockwave multimedia. It is both free and easy to get, and it ships with Windows 95, 98, MacOS, Internet Explorer CD, America Online, and Netscape Navigator. So, you might already have Shockwave on your PC and don't need to do anything special—just enjoy the sites that use it.

If you want to either download the latest Shockwave version, or view a Shockwave site (this also tells you whether you already have Shockwave), perform the following steps:

1. Go to the Macromedia Web site (they make Shockwave) at `www.macromedia.com`.
2. Click the **Shockwave** link on the home page.

148

3. Select **Download Shockwave** if you want to download the latest version; or select **Shocked Site of the Day** if you want to view a Web site that uses Shockwave.

Adobe Acrobat

Created by Adobe Systems, Adobe Acrobat Reader is a software program that lets you view files that are saved as Adobe PDF files. Adobe PDF is a special file format that saves and presents printed material on your computer screen. Unlike the pages on a Web site, Adobe PDF files are exact replicas of printed material, including a table of contents. Acrobat Reader works with your Web browser to present the PDF files right in your browser screen. You can use the controls on the Acrobat Reader software to move through the PDF file, enlarge portions of the copy, search the text, and print the text.

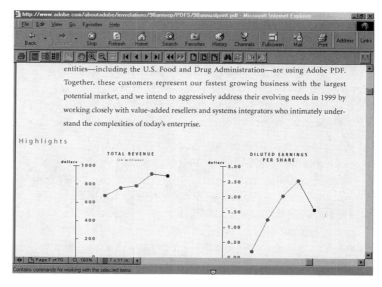

For the latest version of Acrobat Reader, visit **www.adobe.com**, and follow the appropriate links to download it.

Java

Created by Sun Microsystems, Java is a computer language that can create programs (and, just as with any software, the programs can run a wide variety of applications). Java programs run over networks (including the Internet), run on any computer, and do not use a tremendous amount of space. When you visit a Web site that uses Java, the Java program or application downloads and runs on your PC. So, you don't have to download Java specifically. If a Web site uses Java, it usually downloads and runs automatically—you might not even know that Java is being used.

WEB SITE HOSTING AND CREATION

After surfing through several hundred Web sites, you'll get the sudden urge to have your own site—for yourself, your organization, or your company. And why not? Having your own Web site is not that expensive, or difficult—if you know what you're doing. You will discover only two big-picture aspects to having a Web site:

1. Hosting the Web site on a server.
2. Creating (or programming) and updating the site.

Hosting refers to having a company that houses your Web site files (HTML, images, programming) on their computer so that the world can access them. Creating is, of course, the act of putting together your Web site by using the programming languages of the Internet.

This section covers Web site hosting and creation extensively, focusing on the following main topics:

- Basic HTML
- Domain Names
- Free Web Site Creation
- Hosting a Web Site
- HTML Editors and Web Site Creation Software
- Saving a Microsoft PowerPoint Presentation As HTML
- Saving Microsoft Word Files As HTML
- Using AOL to Create a Web Site
- Using GeoCities to Create a Web Site

BASIC HTML

Web pages are created with a simple, versatile program-ming language known as *Hypertext Markup Language*—HTML for short. The emphasis is really on Markup, because that's how you create Web pages—you mark up a document with special HTML codes or tags. You insert these HTML codes around blocks of text in a document to describe how the text displays when the Web page loads.

HTML *tags* consist of a left-angle bracket < followed by the function or directive of the tag and a right-angle bracket >. Beginning and ending tags usually surround the text that you write; a slash / appears just before the directive in the ending tag. Directives are enclosed in brackets <TITLE>. Browsers interpret these tags and directives to determine how to format information and when to start and stop formatting. For example, to make the word "smart" appear in boldface you use this code:

```
<b>smart</b>
```

Within the text on the text file, characters such as the carriage return have no effect. The HTML formatting tags determine when a paragraph occurs. The tags in HTML are not case sensitive—that is, it doesn't matter whether you write the information in uppercase or lowercase letters. Therefore, the tag <Title> is the same as <TITLE>. The Web browser opens the page and interprets HTML commands, formatting each structure in the page. Table 18 offers some basic HTML directives.

Table 18

Basic HTML Directives

HTML Directive	Purpose
TITLE	Gives a title for the page.
H#	Formats a header in larger typeface.
P	Designates the end of a paragraph.
IMG	Points at a picture file to be placed on the page.
A	Creates a hypertext link to another page or resource.
B	Applies boldface formatting.
I	Applies italic formatting.
U	Applies underline formatting.
strong	Makes letters more intense; similar to boldface.

continues

Table 18   Continued

Basic HTML Directives

HTML Directive	Purpose
center	Centers text (and visuals) on the page/document.
HR	Places a rule line (a horizontal line) across the page/document.
LI	An item in a list.
BR	Starts a new line in a paragraph (break).
PRE	Displays the text with the formatting that you use.

Other HTML tags enable you to import media (images, sounds, animation) into the Web page. There are also commands to create links to other Web pages or to send email. Following are a few examples:

HTML Code

```
<a href="http://www.microsoft.com">Microsoft</a>
```

Action

Opens Microsoft Web site

HTML Code

```
<img src=regina.gif>
```

Action

Opens a picture (a gif file) named Regina

HTML Code

```
<a href="mailto:eager@rmi.net">
```

Action

Launches a mail application and places the recipient as
`eager@rmi.net`

DOMAIN NAMES

Your domain name is your Internet Web site address. Most of the free Web hosting services (see "Free Web Site Creation") attach your name to the end of a long URL that has lots of //'s in it. That's great for free, but you might want a shorter name that you can put on a business card and people can remember.

You must register (and pay) for a domain name. You can pay for a two-year registration that can be renewed for another two years. Network Solutions is the company that currently registers most of the domain names (and the important .com names). Network Solutions offers InterNIC registration services.

Most of the great names that end in .com have already been taken. So, your first order of business is to see whether the name you want is available. You could sit at your computer with your browser and type names, such as **www.groovy.com** (this is actually a real address). Unfortunately, this would both take a long time, and you might actually miss the site because a site domain name can be registered, but not yet up-and-running. Better yet go to the InterNIC Web site and perform a quick search.

Following is an overview of the process to locate, register, and activate a new Internet domain name (more detailed instructions to follow):

1. Perform a search to find out whether the domain name that you want is available.
2. Contact your Internet service provider and arrange for domain name service (see the following Note).
3. Review the InterNIC's registration policies and billing procedures.
4. Fill out a registration template at the InterNIC Web site.
5. The template is processed (you are notified if there are any problems).

6. You receive an email from InterNIC that tells you when the process is complete.

7. The information for your new domain is added to InterNIC's whois (the lookup) database (so other people don't register your name).

8. InterNIC sends you an invoice (you can also pay online with a credit card).

9. InterNIC sends you a renewal notice 60 days before the two-year anniversary of the registration.

NOTE

The address of a computer on the Internet is a string of numbers, which is the Internet Protocol address (such as 192.45.24.3). Domain names provide the plain English version. But the Internet uses the numerical address. Therefore, to use domain names, the Internet uses computers known as name servers to translate domain names into the corresponding IP address. This process is known as resolution. Most Internet service providers have name servers. They can provide this important names-to-numbers translation, which is the domain name service. If you don't have domain name service, InterNIC will not process your registration. You will not be able to use your domain name, and other people will not be able to use your domain name to find your site on the Internet. So, this is a very important step.

Getting your Web address (or domain name) involves two processes. First, you need to search for and locate an available name (such as www.yourname.com). Second, you need to formally register this name so that you own it. The following two subsections provide details on each.

Search for Domain Names

To make sure the name you desire is available, you'll need to first search for it. To search for a domain name, perform the following steps:

1. Go to `www.networksolutions.com`.

2. Type your name in the field labeled "Search the database of registered domain names by using WHOIS." (WHOIS is a database of the domain names and who owns them.)

3. Click **Search**.

NOTE

You must type the name with the top-level domain after your name. For example, you could try dog.com or dog.org or dog.net (All taken if you were wondering). You do not need (or use) the http://www for the search.

TIP

You might need to try several names before you find one that is available. Sometimes adding words together (such as dogsmile.com) works. If the name you want is taken you might be able to purchase the rights to buy the name from the current name holder. When you conduct your domain name search at InterNIC, if a name you try has already been taken, the site tells you who owns it and provides an address and phone number.

Register Your Domain Name

When you find a name that is actually available, you need to register it. (As of April 1, 1999, registration fee for domains in .com, .org, or .net, cost $70 (US). This fee covers the costs of the initial registration and updates to your domain name record for two years.) To register your domain name, perform the following steps:

1. Go to **www.networksolutions.com**.
2. Fill in the **Register a Web Address (Domain Name)** form with a name of your choice.
3. Follow the onscreen instructions and complete the forms for your registration.

FREE WEB SITE CREATION

There are some places on the Internet where you can get free Web site service. GeoCities is one of them (see "Using GeoCities to Create a Web Site"). Following are a couple more:

- Nettaxi (**www.nettaxi.com**)
- AngelFire (**www.angelfire.com**)

HOSTING A WEB SITE

You can create the world's best Web site on your hard drive, but, if your computer isn't both set up as a Web server and connected to the Internet (preferably 24 hours a day), then no one can see your work. So, you need to find a company that will host your site.

There are a couple of ways to do this. One is the free approach (hard to beat). Most Internet service providers (for example, AOL) offer a certain amount of hard-disk space on their computers as part of your monthly service fee for access. In many cases, you can use this space to host your Web site (or page). Of course, the old saying "you get what you pay for" is true in the world of the Internet, also. Free probably means that you get limited space for your Web site files (usually 2 or 3 megabytes), the ability to FTP files to your directory, and probably a Web site address that is attached to their domain name (for example, `http://www.isp.com/~yourname`). Not that this is bad for free!

Most ISPs are also willing to sell you more enhanced hosting services. If you want more services, following are a few questions you should ask (especially if you want to shop around for the best deal). Some of these services might be à la carte; others might come with a monthly fee.

- Can they help you register and host your own domain name (`http://www.yourname.com`)?
- How much hard drive space do you get?
- Do you get full FTP access to your directory (to upload and download 24 hours a day)?
- Do they have 24-hour customer support?
- What type of site security do they offer (so no one else can access your Web site files)?
- How fast is their connection to the Internet (T1, T3)? (The faster their access, the faster people can load your pages.)
- Do they back up the files daily?

- Do they have redundant systems? If the computer with your site dies, what happens? (Your site could be down for days without a good redundancy plan.)

- Do they support electronic commerce? If yes, what type? Can you build your own e-commerce store with their system and manage inventory, billing, and product photos?

- What Web site programming do they support (such as CGI-BIN, Cold Fusion, Microsoft ASP)?

- Is there a search engine option for your site (so visitors can search your site)?

HTML EDITORS AND WEB SITE CREATION SOFTWARE

Web pages are created with HTML (Hypertext Markup Language). You will discover that several programs exist that simplify the process of HTML editing, programming, and Web site maintenance. Two of these are Microsoft Word (see "Saving Microsoft Word Files As HTML") and Microsoft PowerPoint (see "Saving a Microsoft PowerPoint Presentation As HTML"). There are others, as well. This section takes a brief look at those—namely:

- HTML Assistant by Brooklyn North Software Works
- FrontPage 98 by Microsoft
- HotDog by Sausage Software

Sometimes you can download a trial version of one of these other programs from their Web site.

At times, it is easier to build your entire site on your PC, and then FTP the programming and files to your host computer. Certain features, such as form submission, require being on the Web server for a real test. Many Webmasters create two sites on their Web server. One is the live site that anyone can visit. The other is a beta site where new content and features are thoroughly tested before they are moved over to the live site.

HTML Assistant by Brooklyn North Software Works is an easy-to-use HTML editor. It is located at www.brooknorth.com and costs approximately $90. Its features include the capability to import word processing files, paste in URLs, position and format graphics, and create backgrounds, tables, forms, frames, and image maps. It also has a spell checker, long filename support, 255 levels of Undo and Redo, support for multimedia tags, Java applets and scripting, and ActiveX objects. (For more information on Java, see Section V, "World Wide Web." ActiveX is a Microsoft standard that creates computer program building blocks called objects.)

FrontPage 98 by Microsoft is for beginners through advanced users. Located at www.microsoft.com, it costs approximately $150. Microsoft FrontPage 98 helps you create WYSIWYG (What You See Is What You Get) frame pages. You can draw HTML tables in a WYSIWYG FrontPage editor. Automatic hyperlink maintenance helps prevent broken links in your site. Collaboration features enable you to work with other people on your Web site. More than 50 FrontPage design themes provide backgrounds, bullets, banners, hyperlinks, and navigation bars across the entire Web site. A Form Save Results Component helps create a form that sends submissions to an email address. And there is support for Dynamic HTML and cascading style sheets.

HotDog by Sausage Software is designed for professionals. You can find it at www.sausage.com and it costs approximately $200. HotDog Professional 5 Webmaster Suite is a code-based editor that supports the Advanced HTML Property Sheet (this provides fast access to every attribute for the current tag), image editing, Web site management, code compilation, and on-the-fly syntax validation.

POWERPOINT PRESENTATIONS AS HTML

With Microsoft PowerPoint, you can save your presentation as a series of Web pages for online viewing of the presentation (with PowerPoint HTML Wizard). The upcoming subsections indicate how to save the PowerPoint presentation as HTML and then how to upload the converted presentation to the Internet.

Save PowerPoint Presentations As HTML

To save your PowerPoint presentation as HTML, perform the following steps:

1. While in PowerPoint with your PowerPoint Presentation open, choose **File**, then **Save As HTML**.

2. The HTML wizard appears.

3. Use the HTML wizard to make selections about your presentation. Following is an overview of the options available as you use the PowerPoint HTML wizard to create your site:

- **Layout Selection**   Design a new layout or use a previously saved one. Choose the onscreen layout for your presentation.

- **Graphic Type**   Select GIF or JPEG images.

- **Graphic Size**   Choose the pixel resolution and onscreen size of the slides.

- **Information Page**   The start page for your presentation. Put in your email address, a home page address if you have one, and whether you want to let viewers download the entire presentation to their PC.

- **Colors and Buttons**   Make selections about the appearance of background, text, links, and buttons.

- **Layout Options**   Decide where you want navigation buttons to appear in the browser window. Determine the Directory where you want the HTML presentation saved.

Upload a Converted Presentation to the Internet

To upload the converted presentation to the Internet, perform the following steps:

1. Find the folder where all the converted files have been saved. The converted files are the HTML files and the GIF or JPEG images that make your presentation work on the Web. In its last step, the PowerPoint HTML Wizard asks you for the directory in which you want to place this folder (such as My Documents). This folder includes image files and HTML files.

2. Upload or FTP all the files from this folder to the server that is hosting your presentation.

NOTE

PowerPoint creates an index file for this presentation. When you upload these files to the server that is hosting your Web pages, the index file replaces any other index file that you might already have. Some Web servers require the index.htm file to be renamed index.html to work.

SAVING MICROSOFT WORD FILES AS HTML

One of the fastest ways to create HTML (for a potential Web page) is to use Microsoft Word. Word converts most formatting, even tables, into HTML. The upcoming subsections offer detailed instruction pertaining to this task as a whole.

Convert a Word File to HTML

To save your word file as HTML, perform the following steps:

1. Open the Word file that you want to convert to HTML.
2. Choose **File**, then **Save As HTML**.
3. Type a filename, choose the directory within which you want to save the file, and click **Save**.

NOTE

After you click Save, the HTML document appears on your screen and you can continue to modify the HTML document. If you use the same filename for your HTML document as for your Word document you have to remember this and decide which one you want to make modifications to.

TIP

If you are going to create several HTML documents and link them together (create a Web site), it is easier to create a new folder on your hard drive to save all the work in one place.

Format Text for HTML

You can use any of the standard Microsoft Word font- and text-style commands to change the appearance of the text. This includes the font, font size, bold, italic, underline, centered, and even color. To format the color of the text, perform the following steps:

1. Open the HTML file that you created when you saved the Word document as HTML (see the previous section).
2. Select the text and click the **Font color button**.
3. Click the color you want the text to be.

Format Background Color

To format the background color, perform the following steps:

1. Open the HTML file that you created when you saved the Word document as HTML (see the section "Convert a Word File to HTML").

2. Click the **Background** color button on the toolbar.

3. Click the color you want the background to be.

Format Horizontal Rules

Applying a horizontal rule displays a horizontal line in the Web page. To format a horizontal line, perform the following steps:

1. Open the HTML file that you created when you saved the Word document as HTML (see the section "Convert a Word File to HTML").

2. Place your cursor where you want the horizontal line to appear in the Web page.

3. Click the **Horizontal Rule button**.

Insert Scrolling Text

To insert scrolling text, perform the following steps:

1. Open the HTML file that you created when you saved the Word document as HTML (see the section "Convert a Word File to HTML").

2. Choose **Insert**, then **Scrolling Text.**

3. Type your text.

4. Customize (format) the scrolling text to your liking.

5. Click **OK**.

Choose the speed for scrolling.　　　Select a background color.

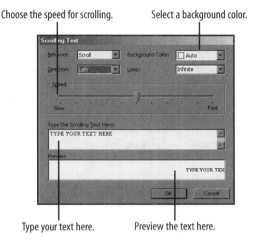

Type your text here.　　　Preview the text here.

Add Pictures to the Page

To add a picture to your page, perform the following steps:

1. Open the HTML file that you created when you saved the Word document as HTML (see the section "Convert a Word File to HTML").

2. Place your cursor where you want the image to appear.

3. Choose **Insert**, then **Picture**, then **From File** (or Clip Art, if you prefer).

4. Select the file, and click **Insert**.

View (and Edit) Source Code of the Document

You might be one of those people who either has a curiosity about the HTML code behind a Web page, or you like to work with HTML codes. You can view the source (HTML) code for your Web document with Microsoft Word. And, you can also directly edit the HTML code if you want to. Perform the following steps:

1. Open the HTML file that you created when you saved the Word document as HTML (see the section "Convert a Word File to HTML").

2. Choose **View**, then HTML source. If you want, you can now edit the HTML code and use **File**, **Save** to save your changes.

3. Click **Exit HTML Source** on the toolbar to see the page again.

NOTE

If you know how to code with HTML, you can add your own HTML code while viewing HTML and then save your additions prior to returning to page view.

View the Document with a Browser

If you want to see what your creation looks like in a Web browser, perform the following steps:

1. With the HTML document open, choose **File**, then **Web Page Preview**.

or

1. With Internet Explorer open, choose **File**, then **Open**.

2. Click **Browse**.

3. Locate your HTML file on your hard drive, and click **OK**.

or

1. With Netscape Navigator open, choose **File**, then **Open Page**.

2. Click **Choose File**.

3. Locate your HTML file on your hard drive, and click **OK**.

Create a Multipage Site

Perhaps you want to create a Web site with multiple pages. First, create all the separate pages that you want by using Word and converting them to HTML. Then, perform the following steps:

1. Open the document that you want to be your start page for the site (the Home Page).

2. Click **Insert**, then **Hyperlink**.

3. Type the path to the Web page you are linking to your home page, or click **Browse** and locate the file on your hard drive.

4. Click **OK**. To add another page from the home page, just repeat this process. You can also open the other pages and add links to them by following these steps.

Publish Your Web Page(s) on the Internet

When you are happy with your work, you can upload it to the Web. If you have an ISP account, they probably enable you to save a certain amount of files on their server. Be sure that you upload all the HTML files and all the picture files for your work.

To upload files to your ISP's Web server, you need to have a File Transfer Protocol program (FTP software). Several popular programs are available. Check with your ISP to see which one they recommend. You can also visit the Ipswitch software Web site (`www.wsftp.com`) and download the free WS-FTP software program. To upload (or FTP) files to the server, you also need to know the following:

- Address for the Web server (such as ftp.rmi.net)
- User ID
- Password
- The directory on the Web server where you will store your Web pages
- The default name for your site's home page (index.html, default.htm, and so on)
- The Web address that people will use to access your pages

Your ISP can answer these questions for you. Some ISPs have specific ways to get through their firewalls (these are security systems to prevent unauthorized access to the computers), so you should ask your ISP whether there are any special instructions for FTPing to the server. After you do have FTP access, you use your FTP software to send files from your hard drive to the Web server.

> **TIP**
>
> When you upload your files to the Internet server that hosts your site, the common default name for a home page is index.html. Be sure that you rename your home page index.html prior to uploading.

USING AOL TO CREATE A WEB SITE

AOL lets members build and maintain a free Web site. AOL's My Place is a storage place for your Web site and other files. My Place provides every AOL member up to 2MB of space for every screen name. Thus, with a maximum of five screen names per account, you have a total of 10MB of space.

You have two choices for creating your site. You can use your own Web-editing tools, create a site on your PC, and then upload these files to AOL's My Place. Or, you can use the AOL Personal Publisher that guides you through the creation of your site. The upcoming subsections offer detailed instruction pertaining to AOL and Web site creation.

Upload Files to My Place

First you use your Web site creation tools (HotDog, FrontPage, Microsoft Word, and so on) to create your Web site pages. Then you upload these files to the AOL Web server so that they become live on the Web. All files you upload to My Place are available to everyone via the Internet. Your Web address is `http://members.aol.com/yourscreenname`. Your start page needs to be an HTML file that is labeled index.html. The only exception is files that you upload to the private directory. If you want to have help on your site, you can allow other people to upload files to your My Place FTPspace. You do this by creating a directory called incoming. To upload a file to My Place, perform the following tasks:

1. Go to Keyword: **My Place**.

Using AOL

2. Click the **My FTPspace** icon. A window that shows the current directories and files in the FTPspace appears.

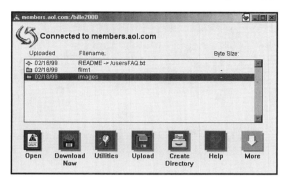

3. Click **Upload**.

4. In the **Remote FileName** field, enter a name for the file. The name should be the same as the name of the HTML file that you are uploading, and the home page needs to be labeled index.html.

5. Identify the type of file for upload, binary, or ASCII. Files are binary unless they are text documents. Binary files contain information that does not consist of text— such as a spreadsheet, image, or sound file. Your graphic images and HTML files are binary files.

6. Click **Continue**.

7. In the Upload File window, click **Select File**. Select the file you want to upload from your hard drive.

8. In the Upload File window, click **Send File**. The file uploads to your FTPspace.

NOTE

If you are creating HTML files or uploading multimedia files for a Web site, you must retain the exact name of your HTML documents. For example, if you upload an image that appears on a home page ("sunset.gif"), you must place "sunset.gif" in the Remote Name field without the quotation marks.

Use the AOL Personal Publisher to Create a Web Page

AOL's Personal Publisher allows you the means by which to create your own site within AOL. It offers templates from which to choose as a starting point, and then provides further options for customizing colors, text, and images (lots of choices from Auto to Film to Science). The process is really point-and-click and you can have your site up and running in less than one hour. To create a Web page by using AOL Personal Publisher, perform the following steps:

1. From within AOL, click the **My AOL** button on the toolbar.
2. Select **Personal Publisher**.
3. Click **Create a Page**.
4. Select a Template (from the scrolling list) and click Use This Template.
5. Customize the content and click **Next** as you make each selection (for example, color).

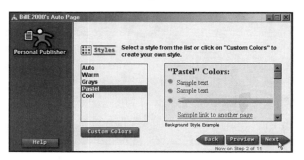

6. Click **Publish** at the end of the template process.

View Your Web Page

After you publish your site, you can view it with any Web browser (including AOL's). The Web address for your site is `http://members.aol.com/yourscreenname/templatename` (where *yourscreenname* is your AOL screen name and *templatename* is the name of the template you selected). If you go to My FTP Space, you will notice that AOL creates a directory with the name of the template and places the index.html file in that directory.

Edit Your Web Page with Personal Publisher

To edit your Web page with AOL's Personal Publisher, perform the following steps:

1. From within AOL, click the **My AOL** button on the toolbar.
2. Select **Personal Publisher**.
3. Click the **Edit/View My Page** button.
4. Select the page or file you want to edit by clicking it, and click **Edit**.
5. Use the Personal Publisher options to edit the page.
6. Click **Publish** to update the page.

> **NOTE**
>
> Whether you use your own HTML editor or type HTML code, you can no longer use the AOL Personal Publisher as a tool for page editing.

Add Pages and Modify Your Site

You can continue to use the AOL's Personal Publisher (see previous sections) to create multiple pages. Then, when you create or publish two or more pages, you can create a menu to link the pages together to create a site.

Explore Hometown AOL

Hometown AOL is AOL's Web community. There are literally thousands and thousands of Web pages and sites created by AOL members. The sites are placed in categories such as Careers, Education, Entertainment, and so on. You can list your created Web site in the community so that other people can find it. You select a category, and your home page is listed and keyword searchable. You can add your pages to the community, or visit other users' pages. To access Hometown AOL and add your pages, perform the following steps:

1. Go to Keyword: **Hometown**. (Type Hometown in the address field under the toolbar and click **Go**.)

2. To add your page(s), click **Add Pages**. This opens an easy-to-use wizard that helps you add or edit your listing in Hometown.

USING GEOCITIES TO CREATE A WEB SITE

Yahoo! acquired GeoCities (**www.geocities.com**). Why? Because with more than 3.5 million sites authored and hosted on GeoCities, the company has created one of the Web's largest communities. GeoCities Web-based publishing tools enable nontechnical users to create, publish, and update content on the Web. You must register to become a user, or as they are called on the site, a Homesteader. Indeed, the 3.5 million GeoCities Homesteaders have created more than 32 million pages of personalized Web content! GeoCities offers both free sites and sites with advanced features such as additional storage space and electronic commerce. You receive a site with 11MB of space, subdirectories, and a set of Web-publishing tools at no cost to you. The upcoming subsections offer detailed instruction pertaining to GeoCities and Web site creation.

Get Started (Become a Homesteader)

To create a Web site using GeoCities, the first thing you must do is become a member, a Homesteader. To do so, perform the following steps:

1. Go to the GeoCities home page at **www.geocities.com**.

2. Click **Join**. Follow the onscreen instructions to get your membership for a free personal home page. You have to answer a few questions about your address, age, email, and you also have to agree to the content guidelines and terms of service.

Create a Page

Before you can create your page, you must become a member (see the previous section). To create a page from which to start through GeoCities, perform the following steps:

1. Go to GeoCities (**www.geocities.com**) and click the **Members Area** link.

2. Enter your member name and password (which GeoCities emailed to you after you registered).

3. Click **Members Work on Your Site** button.

4. Click **GeoBuilder Go** button (this opens the GeoCities site builder space).

5. Click the **New** button located in the lower-left corner of the toolbar (at the bottom of the screen). A pop-up window asks you to select one of the GeoCities page templates.

6. Click a template to select it, and then click **Create**. If you select a blank template, you start with a completely blank screen upon which you build your page. At this point, you are just beginning to create your GeoCities Web site. The upcoming subsections provide information on modifying, previewing, and saving your site.

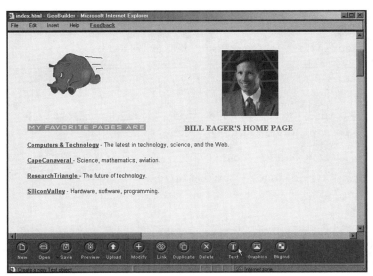

Add Text

To add text to your newly created page (see the previous section), perform the following tasks:

1. From within a GeoCities page, click the **Text** button on the toolbar.

2. Type your text in the pop-up window.

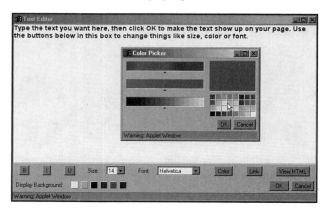

3. Make any text selections (such as color, font, size).
4. Click **OK**.

TIP

You can type HTML tags directly into a text object.

Change Text

To alter the text in any way on a GeoCities-created Web page, perform the following steps:

1. Double-click the text.
2. Type changes in the pop-up text window.
3. Click **OK**.

Move Text

To move text within a GeoCities-created Web page, perform the following steps:

1. Click the text.
2. Hold down the mouse key and drag the text.

Add Graphics

To add a graphic to your GeoCities-created Web page, perform the following steps:

1. Click the **Graphics** button on the toolbar (a pop-up window appears).

2. Click a category of graphics (such as Buttons or Clipart). Links to various graphics appear in the center frame.

3. Click a link to see what the graphic looks like (it appears in the far-right frame).

4. Click the graphic to place it onto the page.

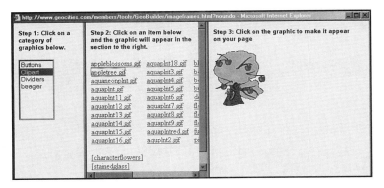

Add Graphics from Your Hard Drive

To add a graphic from your hard drive to your GeoCities-created Web page, perform the following steps:

1. Click **Upload** on the toolbar.

2. Enter a filename or click the **Browse** button to locate the image on your hard drive.

3. Click **Open** and the image is uploaded and appears on your page.

Change the Size of Something on the Page

To alter the size of any items on your GeoCities-created Web page, perform the following steps:

1. Click once on the item you want to resize. A blue border appears next to the item, and a little red square appears in the lower-right corner.

2. Click the red square, holding down the mouse key.

3. Move your mouse to resize the item.

Create Links

After you start building your GeoCities Web page, you might want to link text or images to other Web pages. To do so, perform the following steps:

1. Click the item you want to link.

2. Click **Link** on the toolbar.

3. A pop-up window appears. Type the URL for the page you want to link.

4. Click **OK**.

TIP

You can use GeoBuilder to import existing Web pages. Use the **File/Open** menu item to import files from your home directory, or **File/Import** to import them from other locations on the Web.

Save Your Page

When you have finalized your GeoCities page and you want to save it, perform the following step:

1. Click the **Save** button on the toolbar.

NOTE

The Preview button on the toolbar opens the page in a browser. When you save a page, GeoCities shows you the URL for that page. I recommend writing it down. To make a page your home page, label it index.html. To create a rich site, you create multiple pages and link to them from your home page.

WEB RESOURCES: FIND IT ON THE INTERNET

What is the least expensive flight from Denver to Zurich? Where can you get a map and driving directions for a business meeting? What are financial analysts saying about that Internet stock that you want to buy? Does your old college roommate have an email address?

The world is full of information, and the Internet is becoming a terrific tool for both finding the information you need and acting on it. Not only can you conduct online research about stocks, you also can buy them. Airlines provide both the details about flights and online ordering. This section provides both quick-reference information and tips for locating the information you need, as well as overviews of some of the most useful sites on the Internet.

Specifically, this section addresses the following main topic areas:

- Search Engines
- Audio and Video on the Web
- Finding and Using Maps on the Net
- Finding Businesses on the Net
- Finding People on the Net
- News on the Net
- Stock and Finance on the Net
- Travel Information on the Net

SEARCH ENGINES

There are more than 30 million Web pages to visit! This, of course, is both a blessing and a curse. Lots of Web pages translates into lots of information—some useful, some not.

That's one reason the *search engine* Web sites have become very popular. These sites help you sort through the mountains of information on the Internet. Actually, search engine is a general-use term that covers a variety of activities. First, intelligent software programs scour the Web on a regular basis collecting information about existing Web sites. This information is then compiled into a database that you can access—and search.

You connect to a search engine just as you do any other Web resource, by entering the site's Web address (URL) into your browser. Table 19 lists some of the most popular search engines.

Table 19

Popular Search Engines

Search Engine	Web Site
AltaVista	`www.altavista.com`
Excite	`www.excite.com`
Go	`www.go.com`
HotBot	`www.hotbot.com`
InfoSeek	`www.infoseek.com`
Lycos	`www.lycos.com`
Snap	`www.snap.com`
Yahoo!	`www.yahoo.com`
Webcrawler	`www.webcrawler.com`

Most search engines provide two methods for you to locate other Web sites that have the information you need:

1. Weave through subject-based categories and subcategories to locate what you want. For example, at Yahoo!, start by clicking a category called Arts and Humanities, which opens several choices including Visual Arts. Click this, and you get choices including Photography, which opens new choices, including Photojournalism. Then you get a list of Web sites. So, you narrow your search by selecting (and selecting) categories within categories.

2. Type a keyword or phrase and search the database. From the home page of the search site, type a word or phrase that identifies what you're looking for. Perhaps antique cars. Then click a Search button, and the site presents a list of sites that should match your interest.

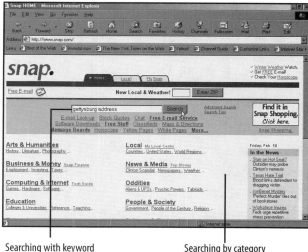

Searching with keyword   Searching by category

The end result of a search is a list of Web sites. With a keyword search, the search engine hunts for sites that contain the word or words that you type. If you do a keyword search, the list is your *results page.* You can then click links to visit these sites. All too often a keyword search gives you a list of hundreds, even thousands of sites to visit. Following are a few tips to make your search more effective. These tips should work with any search site that you use:

- Put quotation marks around your keywords so that the search engine looks only for sites that exactly match your phrase.

- Use several search engines with the same keyword.

- If you get a results page with too many Web sites, try narrowing your search. For example, Australian shepherd breeders in Colorado is more precise than dog breeder.

- See whether the description of a Web page on the results page also includes a date for the Web page (you can sometimes eliminate information that is several years old).

- Most search engines offer an advanced-searching link on the home page. You can narrow your search criteria.

- If you get a results page that has lots of useful links, save the page on your hard drive (see Section V, "The World Wide Web"). You can later open this page to continue examining the sites without redoing the search.

AUDIO AND VIDEO ON THE WEB

Now, when you tell people that the Web is music to your ears, you can really mean it. Audio (and video) is becoming a standard aspect of many Web sites. You can send and receive Web greeting cards that have music soundtracks. You can listen to news broadcasts. You can download both samples and entire songs from your favorite artists.

There are a couple of different types of audio (and video) files on the Internet. Some audio/video files need to be entirely downloaded to your PC before you can play them. Microsoft Windows Media Player is a software program built into Windows 95 and 98, and it automatically launches and plays the audio and video file types in the upcoming list. (This list is really just for reference to show you how many different types of file formats there are on the Internet for audio and video.) Media Player launches and plays the file when you double-click a link on a Web page that points to a file that has one of the following extensions:

- **Windows Media Formats file extensions** .asf, .asx
- **RealNetworks, RealAudio, and RealVideo (version 4.0 or earlier) file extensions** .ra, .ram, .rm, .rmm
- **Audio Visual Interleave (AVI) file extension** .avi
- **Moving Pictures Experts Group (MPEG) file extensions** .mpg, .mpeg, .m1v, .mp2, .mpa, .mpe
- **Musical Instrument Digital Interface (MIDI) file extensions** .mid, .rmi
- **Apple QuickTime®, Macintosh® AIFF Resource file extensions** .qt, .aif, .aifc, .aiff, .mov

- **Sun Microsystems and NeXT file extensions**   .au, .snd
- **Audio for Windows file extension**   .wav

TIP

Sometimes Web sites have links only to audio/video files and you really won't know how long it takes before they completely download and you can watch or listen. The better sites put a file size next to the audio or video, so you can decide whether you want to wait. For reference, a 1MB file can take about four to six minutes to download with a 56Kbps modem. If you get bored waiting, you can always cancel the download or launch a second browser window and do other work while the audio/video loads.

Or, if you don't like waiting, try streaming audio or video files to your PC. What does this mean? Instead of supplying an entire file (a package) to download to your PC, a streaming audio or video file is sent continuously in little pieces. The result is that you can begin to listen to the audio or video in as few as five seconds, even with a 28.8Kbps modem.

Real Networks was one of the first companies to offer streaming media. Today more than 50 million users have registered to use the RealPlayer software, and every week, more than 145,000 hours of live sports, music, news, and entertainment are broadcast over the Internet with RealSystem technology. Go to `www.real.com` to download either the free RealPlayer or the moderately priced RealPlayer Plus player.

After you install RealPlayer on your PC, it works with your Web browser and launches automatically when you click a link to any Real Networks streaming audio or video that is on a Web site (and there are a lot—see the following list). There are links to other samples at the Real Networks Web site. For complete instructions on how you can get the RealPlayer software, see the appropriate subsection in Section V, "World Wide Web."

Table 20 provides a list of sites by category where you can find streaming audio and video. After you install RealPlayer on your PC, you can explore these sites and try links to various streaming audio and video.

Table 20

Web Sites That Offer Streaming Audio/Video

Audio/Video Site	Web Address
News	
ABC News Radio	`www.abcnewsradio.com`
Bloomberg	`www.bloomberg.com`
Internet News	`stream.internet.com`
National Public Radio	`www.npr.org`
Music	
CD Now	`www.cdnow.com`
Broadcast.com	`www.broadcast.com`
Live Concerts.Com	`www.liveconcerts.com`
Radio and Television Stations	
RealNetworks	`www.timecast.com/`
	`stations/index.html`

continues

184

Table 20   Continued
Web Sites That Offer Streaming Audio/Video

Audio/Video Site	Web Address
Science and Technology	
CMPNet Radio	`www.cmpnet.com/radio`
Healthtalk Interactive	`www.htinet.com`
Sports	
ESPN	`http://espn.go.com/liveradiotv`
SportsWorld	`www.sportsworld.com/` `sportsradio.stm`

FINDING AND USING MAPS ON THE NET

You've never been to the hospital. Your new friend invites you over for dinner. The job interview is in a part of town you're not familiar with. You need a map. The Net is an excellent resource for getting your hands on the map you need.

The upcoming subsections offer instructions for acquiring and using maps via the Internet.

Use Mapquest to Acquire a Map

Mapquest (`www.mapquest.com`) is a Web site that offers a way to acquire a map for an area when you have an address (including city and state, of course). To use this service to acquire a map, perform the following steps:

1. Go to the Mapquest site by entering its Web site address (URL) in the Address field of your browser (`www.mapquest.com`).

2. From the home page click **Maps**.

3. Fill in the address, city, and state fields for the location for which you want to obtain a map.

4. Click **Get Map**. Mapquest delivers a new page with the map you need. You can zoom in and out of the map to change scale by using the zoom toolbar on the left side of the screen.

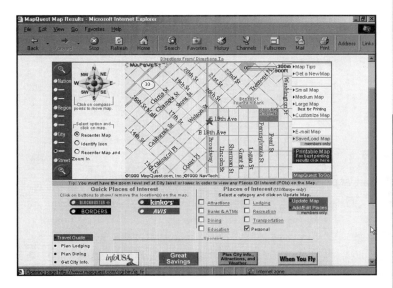

Use Mapquest to Locate Lodging, Restaurants, and More

Mapquest also can help you locate banks, ATMs, restaurants, lodging, and recreational opportunities. After you retrieve a map (see the previous section), perform the following steps:

1. On the page of the retrieved map, scroll down to the section labeled "Places of Interest."

2. Click the check box next to one of the categories.

3. Click **Update Map** to show the locations on your map.

4. Click **Show 5 Closest Selected POIs** (Points Of Interest) to retrieve address and phone information.

Use Mapquest to Email a Map

You have to join Mapquest to receive some additional map functionality (it's free). To join Mapquest, simply click the Free Membership link on the home page and follow the registration steps. One nice feature is that you can create a map, and then send an email message that contains a hyperlink to a Web page with that map. Doing this is a great way to help a friend who has Net access but is unfamiliar with Mapquest. After you are a member, and after you create a map (see the section "Use Mapquest to Acquire a Map"), perform the following steps:

1. Click the **Email Map** link beside the map.

2. Type appropriate information in the fields for email to: address, from, and subject.

3. Click **Email Map**. An email with a link to the map is now sent to your friend.

Save a Map with Mapquest

This is another membership feature of Mapquest. You can save a map you've created (see the section "Use Mapquest to Acquire a Map"). There are actually two ways to do so. The first method saves the map as a GIF file on your hard drive. You can always go back and open this file with your browser. The second method saves the map at the Mapquest server. When you are online, access your member space, and then retrieve any of the maps that you have saved.

To save a map by using the first method (hard drive), perform the following steps:

1. Right-click the map you've created.

2. Choose **Save Picture As**.

3. Type a filename, the directory within which you want to save it, and click **Save**.

To save a map by using the second method (Mapquest server), perform the following steps (remember you must register for this free service before you can save anything— see the previous section):

1. Open your member space (Mapquest provides members with a personal URL or Web address that you receive via email after you complete the registration process). For convenience, you can add this URL to your browser's favorites or bookmarks for easy access.

2. Create the map you want.

3. Click the **Save/Load** map link next to the map.

4. If you are saving a map, type a map name and click
   Save Map. The map is now saved at the Mapquest Web
   server.

Retrieve a Map Saved with Mapquest

To retrieve a map you've saved with Mapquest (see the
previous section), perform the following steps:

1. Access your Mapquest personal page (the URL will be
   emailed to you after registration).

2. You will find a list of saved maps in a pull-down menu.
   Select the map you want, and click the **Go** button.

3. Your saved map appears onscreen.

FINDING BUSINESSES ON THE NET

How many times have you wanted to locate a specific business? Sure, you can use your local Yellow Pages book. But
you might not receive the most current information. And,
if the business you need is in another city or state—good
luck. Web business directories offer a valuable service with
fast access to addresses, phone numbers, maps, and more.
The upcoming sections offer instruction for using two such
directories.

Use GTE SuperPages

GTE SuperPages (located at `www.superpages.com`) is basically a nationwide listing of companies. Results pages (of a
search) offer address information, phone numbers, and
online maps. To utilize this service, perform the following
steps:

1. Go to the GTE SuperPages site by entering its Web site
   address (URL) in the Address field of your browser
   (`www.superpages.com`).

2. On the simple search form at this site's home page,
   enter the type of business you want to find in the
   Category field (anything), or enter the specific name
   of a business in the Business Name field.

188

3. Enter the name of a city in the City field and select a state from the pull-down menu.

4. Click **Find It**. If you have missed any information that the site needs, it tells you which fields have to be re-entered. Otherwise, you get a new page with a list of relevant categories (for example, if you type paint—you would get a list that includes auto painting).

5. Double-click one of the subcategories and SuperPages returns a list of businesses with addresses and phone numbers that are in that subcategory.

TIP

Can't think of a category? Click the Top Categories link on the home page (next to Enter Category field) to get a laundry list of business categories.

Use BigYellow.com

BigYellow claims to offer information on 16 million U.S. business listings. It provides a way of searching for businesses by category or by name, by city and state. To use this service, perform the following steps:

1. Go to the BigYellow site by entering its Web site address (URL) in the Address field of your browser (`www.bigyellow.com`).

2. At a minimum, type either a category or business name in the appropriate (and respective) field(s) and also the state.

3. Click **Find It**. BigYellow returns a list of categories or businesses that match your search criteria. If you get a page of categories, then you click a category to get a list of businesses.

FINDING PEOPLE ON THE NET

With some 50 million plus Internet users, there is a good chance that many of your friends, family, and business associates have an email address. But, if they haven't given you this address, how do you find them? Well, there are Web sites that are the equivalent of an online phone book. You can find email addresses, home addresses, and phone numbers.

NOTE

Sometimes you'll receive several email addresses from an individual. That person might actually have several email addresses, or it might be that he switched service providers and the old listings are still in circulation.

TIP

Sometimes people are listed with their given names. So, for someone you know as Bill, try William.

The upcoming subsections offer instruction for finding people on the Net by way of four different Web sites.

Use Switchboard.com

Switchboard.com (located at `www.switchboard.com`) is a great site to find both email addresses and other information about people. To find a person, including information about their address and phone number, perform the following steps:

1. Go to the Switchboard site by entering its Web site address (URL) in the Address field of your browser (`www.switchboard.com`).
2. Click **Find a Person** at the home page.
3. Enter at least a last name for a search. If you can also add a first name, city, and state, your search is more precise.
4. Click **Search**. A results page provides a list of the people that match your search. The list includes a street address and phone number. Common names such as Smith usually give you more than one person.

To find an email address, perform the following steps:

1. Click **Find Email** at the home page.
2. Type a first and last name (only last name required).
3. Click **Search**. The results page shows a list of people, with their email addresses, that matches your search. Common names such as Smith usually give you more than one person.

Use US WEST Dex

Even though U.S. West (located at `www.uswestdex.com`) is a Regional Bell Operating Company, its online site offers listings for individuals in all 50 states. To find a residential listing with address and phone number, perform the following steps:

1. Go to the US WEST Dex site by entering its Web site address (URL) in the Address field of your browser (`www.uswestdex.com`).
2. At the home page, click **Residential White Pages** icon.
3. Type at least a last name.
4. Select a **state**.
5. Click **Submit Search**. A results page provides a list of the people that match your search. The list includes a street address and phone number. Common names such as Smith usually give you more than one person.

FINDING PEOPLE ON THE NET

Use Bigfoot

You can use a service called Bigfoot (located at
`www.bigfoot.com`) to find email addresses or white pages
(listings of street addresses and phone numbers). To do so,
perform the following steps:

1. Go to the Bigfoot site by entering its Web site
   address (URL) in the Address field of your browser
   (`www.bigfoot.com`).
2. At the home page, type a full name in the Name field.
3. Select Email, White pages, or both.
4. Click **Search**. A search results page shows matches for
   names, email, street, and phone numbers.

Use Yahoo! People Search

Yahoo! People Search (located at `www.people.yahoo.com`)
offers a one-page form that enables you to search for both
email and white page listings (street addresses and phone
numbers). To do so, perform the following steps:

1. Go to the Yahoo! People Search site by entering its
   Web site address (URL) in the Address field of your
   browser (`www.people.yahoo.com`).

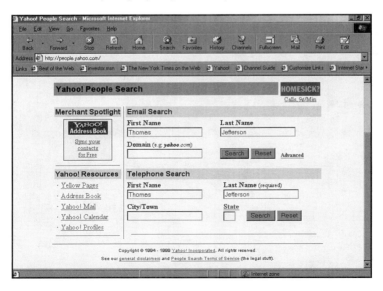

2. At the home page, type a first and last name to find an email address (domain names—the name of the ISP for the person—is an optional field). For a white pages search, put in first name, last name, and city and state.

3. Click **Search**. A search results page shows matches for names, email, street, and phone numbers.

NEWS ON THE NET

Like the world, the Internet is "on" 24 hours a day. And you can access up-to-the-minute news at a variety of locations. In fact, there are thousands and thousands of newspapers, and radio and television stations (the traditional news outlets) that now have Web sites.

Table 21 shows some of the best national news Web sites.

Table 21

National News Web Sites

Television News	Web Site
ABC	`abcnews.go.com`
Bloomberg	`www.bloomberg.com`
CBS	`www.cbs.com/navbar/news.html`
CNN	`www.cnn.com`
CNN en Español	`www.cnnenespanol.com`
FOX	`www.foxnews.com`
MSNBC	`www.msnbc.com`
Radio News	
NPR	`www.npr.org`
MIT Station List	`wmbr.mit.edu/stations/list.html`
Newspaper News	
American City Business Journals	`www.amcity.com`
The New York Times	`www.nytimes.com`
USA Today	`www.usatoday.com`
Wall Street Journal	`www.wsj.com`
Washington Post	`www.washingtonpost.com`

There also are useful international news sites—from all over the world. Many offer English-language news; many are in the language of their country (see Table 22).

Table 22

International News Sites

Country and Periodical	Web Site
Argentina	
La Nación	www.lanacion.com.ar
Brazil	
Net Estado	www.estado.com.br
Canada	
Canadian Broadcasting	www.radio.cbc.ca
Calgary Herald	www.calgaryherald.com
Chile	
El Mercurio	www.mercurio.cl
China	
South China Morning Post	www.scmp.com
Egypt	
Egyptian Gazette	www.egy.com
France	
Les Echos	www.lesechos.fr
Germany	
Die Zeit	www2.zeit.de/zeit
India	
Hindustan Times	www.hindustantimes.com
Japan	
Asahi	www.asahi.com/english/english.html
New Zealand	
Allied Press	www.alliedpress.co.nz
Russia	
St. Petersburg Times	www.sptimes.ru
Saudi Arabia	
Al-Jazirah	www.al-jazirah.com
Spain	
El Periódico	www.elperiodico.es

International News Sites

Country and Periodical	Web Site
Switzerland	
Tages Anzeiger	`www.tages-anzeiger.ch`
United Kingdom	
British Broadcasting	`www.bbc.co.uk`
The Times of London	`www.the-times.co.uk`

To reach any of these national or international sites, simply enter its Web site address in the Address field of your browser.

> **TIP**
>
> There is also a very good chance that your local television, radio stations, and newspapers have Web sites. Go to your favorite search engine and type their name or station call letters.

STOCK AND FINANCE ON THE NET

The Internet has changed the way that people research and invest in the stock market. With a few clicks of your mouse, you can retrieve current stock quotes or you can get detailed research information, analyst recommendations, SEC filings, and company financial results.

Online trading rose 34% in the fourth quarter of 1998, according to a report by Credit Suisse First Boston Corporation. In fact, online trades accounted for almost 14% of the stock market trading. The top five online brokers were Charles Schwab, Waterhouse Investor Services, Etrade, Datek, and Fidelity. Every day, there were approximately 340,000 online trades. The Nasdaq Stock market realized a 14% increase in online trades, and the NYSE had a 1.5% increase.

Table 23 identifies some of the Web sites that offer both financial information and online trading.

Table 23

Finance Online

Online Stock Trading	Web Site
Charles Schwab	`www.charlesschwab.com`
Datek	`www.datek.com`
Etrade	`www.etrade.com`
Fidelity	`www.fidelity.com`
Waterhouse	`www.waterhouse.com`
Financial Research	**Web Site**
Microsoft Investor	`investor.msn.com`
Motley Fool	`www.fool.com`
NASDAQ	`www.nasdaq.com`
Yahoo! Quotes	`quote.yahoo.com`

The Nasdaq stock exchange has created a wonderful Web site that has lots of information about publicly traded companies. The following two subsections give you more details on using Nasdaq specifically.

Use Nasdaq to Gather Information (Get the Symbol)

The Nasdaq Web site (located at `www.nasdaq.com`) offers a wealth of financial information at no charge. In addition to stock prices, the Nasdaq Web site offers volume, price charting, SEC (Securities and Exchange Commission) filing, news, analyst information, P/E (price to earnings) ratios, and other information about securities. To find out information about publicly traded companies or mutual funds, you need to know their stock symbol. If you know it already, you can move on to the next section. To look up a symbol for a stock or mutual fund, perform the following steps:

1. Go to the Nasdaq site by entering its Web site address (URL) in the Address field of your browser (`www.nasdaq.com`).

2. From the home page, click the **Use Symbol Look Up** link.

3. Type a name (or partial name) of the company or mutual fund you are looking for.

4. Click **Symbol Look Up**. The results page shows you the company or mutual fund stock symbol.

Get Stock Quotes at Nasdaq

After you have the symbol for the fund you're interested in (see the previous section), you can use it at the Nasdaq site to get the financial information you're seeking. Perform the following steps:

1. From the Nasdaq home page (**www.nasdaq.com**), type the symbol of a stock or mutual fund.

2. Click the option button for stocks or mutual funds.

3. Click Get FlashQuotes to retrieve last sale, net change, % change, and share volume. Click Get InfoQuotes for more detailed coverage.

STOCK AND FINANCE ON THE NET

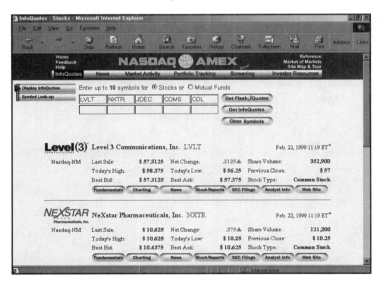

TRAVEL INFORMATION ON THE NET

The Internet is changing the way many people research their travel plans and purchase travel arrangements. You can find a tremendous amount of online information about any travel destination that you can think of—from a romantic spa in Italy to a jungle safari in South America. And, whether your plans are for personal pleasure or for business travel, the Internet can save you time and money. Surf the Net and cruise the world.

There are great Web sites that can help you get discount travel tickets and learn about places you want to travel. The following subsections provide overviews of some of these sites.

Use the Net to Acquire Airline and Flight Information

Many airlines have tied their huge computer systems into the Internet. As a result, you can look up flight options, flight information, book your tickets, and make seat assignments.

The Internet is helping both consumers and the travel industry. Unlike any other industry, every day the travel industry loses money on airline seats that are empty when the plane takes off, or hotel rooms that are empty at the end of the day. As a result, many companies are offering last minute *e-fares* (electronic fares), where you can purchase discount tickets or arrangements just prior to the date they expire. If you want a bargain, look for links on airline Web sites to e-fares. Table 24 provides the Web addresses for a large number of airlines.

Table 24

Airline Web Sites

Airline	Web Site
Air Canada	`www.aircanada.ca`
Air France	`www.airfrance.com`
American Airlines	`www.americanairlines.com`

Airline	Web Site
British Airways	`www.british-airways.com`
Continental	`www.flycontinental.com`
Delta	`www.deltaairlines.com`
Frontier	`www.frontierairlines.com`
Iberia	`www.iberia.com`
Lufthansa	`www.lufthansa.com`
Northwest	`www.nwa.com`
Mexicana	`www.mexicana.com.mx`
SouthWest	`www.southwest.com`
Swiss Air	`www.swissair.com`
TWA	`www.twa.com`
United Airlines	`www.ual.com`

Explore Travel Sites

To make your life even easier, several sites offer full-service information related to travel planning and reservations. These sites increasingly offer details about destinations, provide travel tips, and have the capability to research and purchase airline tickets, hotel reservations, car rentals, and other travel services. Table 25 lists some of the larger travel sites.

Table 25

Internet Travel Sites

Travel Site	Web Site
Microsoft Expedia	`expedia.msn.com`
Travelocity	`www.travelocity.com`
Travel Zoo	`www.travelzoo.com`
The Trip.Com	`www.thetrip.com`
Preview Travel	`www.previewtravel.com`

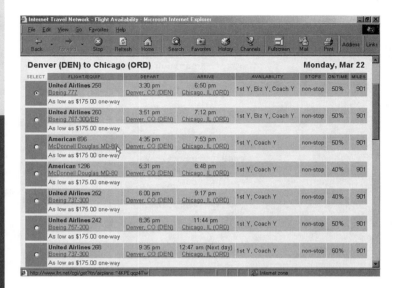

Find and Use Travel Resources

The following World Wide Web sites offer a variety of useful information ranging from travel advisories to health tips, to travel tours. Try them all.

Lonely Planet

Web site: **www.lonelyplanet.com**
Well known for their in-depth travel books, this Web site offers information about destinations, health tips, and many useful articles.

National Tour Association

Web site: **www.ntaonline.com**
National Tour Association is a great site to learn about travel opportunities. From the home page, you can select a travel region and a type of travel—from adventure to cruises to national parks—and retrieve a list of tour packages from hundreds of tour companies.

Steve Kropla's Travel Resources

Web site: **www.kropla.com**

Planning an overseas trip? How about a guide on electrical power, how to plug in your modem, international dialing codes, a world television guide, or travel photo galleries to get you started.

Travel Source

Web site: **www.travelsource.com**

Talk about links! Whether your travel tastes run from yacht charters, golf getaways, guest ranches, honeymoon specials, wine tours, bed-and-breakfast lodging, ecotours, or safaris. This site connects you to the information (and sites) that you need.

U.S. State Department

Web site: **travel.state.gov**

Travel advisories, passport and visa information, money information, U.S. embassies, and consulates worldwide are available on this Web site.

INDEX

D

G

INDEX

217

INDEX

INDEX

T

Y-Z